# Lifeworks

**Summer 1994**

**Volume 84
Number 2**

## Poetry & Reviews

## Endstops

*Cover illustrations by Nicola Jennings*

# CONTENTS

**Editor
Peter Forbes**

**Assistant Editor
Kevan Johnson**

# *Society needs Poetry:* JOIN *the* Poetry Society

**If you write, read, teach or promote poetry, join the Society to develop your knowledge and enjoyment of Britain's most buoyant and participatory artform.**

## *You Will Receive ...*

**POETRY NEWS.** Our new look quarterly newsletter packed with opportunities, ideas and comment. Special issues and supplements will focus on poetry and education, libraries, festivals and new writers.

**POETRY REVIEW,** Britain's leading poetry magazine: 'essential reading for anyone who wants to keep up to date with new poetry. It's the magazine which readers of poetry can't do without.' **– Douglas Dunn, Whitbread Prize Winner**

## *Discounts On ...*

**THE NATIONAL POETRY COMPETITION.** This is open to all – with thirteen cash prizes totalling £5,250 – and has built up a remarkable track record for discovering new talent and affirming the reputations of established names. Past prizewinners include Tony Harrison, Carol Ann Duffy, and Jo Shapcott. Last year's winner, Sam Gardner, was a newcomer to poetry, unknown – until he won £3,000 and saw his poem published by the *Guardian*.

**THE SCRIPT**, a unique service to all those who write poetry. Fill out a questionnaire specially devised to help you think about how and why you write, then send it in with a sample of your poetry for a 'diagnosis' from a skilled professional poet and a 'prescription' of new ideas and further reading.

**POETRY READINGS**, talks and events around the UK.

**INFORMATION & IMAGINATION SEMINARS:** seminars, fact sheets, training courses for teachers, librarians, promoters, poets and all those who love poetry.

## HELPING POETRY THRIVE IN BRITAIN TODAY

### MEMBERSHIP RATES

| | |
|---|---|
| UK Individuals | £24 ☐ |
| UK Concessionary rate (Pensioners, Students, UB40) | £18 ☐ |
| UK Institutions | £30 ☐ |
| European Union | £30 ☐ |
| Rest of world  (surface) | £30 ☐ |
| "        "      (airmail) | £40 ☐ |
| Life membership  (UK only) | £250 ☐ |

Teachers/students: Please tick if you want to be included on the Education mailing list ☐

I wish to make a donation to the Poetry Society of

£10 ☐      £20 ☐ £50       ☐      £100 ☐

I enclose a cheque for £_____
Please debit my Access/Visa account
expiry date_____
Card No.

| | | | | | | | | | | | | | | | | |
|--|--|--|--|--|--|--|--|--|--|--|--|--|--|--|--|--|

Name _____

Address_____

_____

_____

Please send  coupon to:
Membership Secretary, Poetry Society, 22 Betterton St, London WC2H 9BU

**PHOTOCOPY THIS FORM**

# Auden: One Poem & the Jackpot

**I**t is often said that when poetry tangles with the other arts it slinks off with its tail between its legs. Auden's 'Funeral Blues', used as a funeral oration in the Andie McDowell/Hugh Grant film *Four Weddings and a Funeral*, is the exception. The poem is beautifully read by John Hannah but the man he was mourning, played by Simon Callow, has not made the sort of impression that would account for the audience's reaction: it is clearly the poem that precipitates them into full-blown weepie mode.

In America, where the film is a huge success, it has launched an Auden cult. Random House, Auden's US publisher, had not regarded the poet as a major property until the film. A booklet of ten of Auden's more songlike lyrics sold fast and led to interest in Auden's work as a whole. James Fenton, in the *Independent*, has described all this and the interesting background of the poem. The first two stanzas originally appeared with three completely different following ones in the Auden/Isherwood play, *The Ascent of F6*. In this original version the man lamented is a leader, a public figure, with a hint of 30s fascism, and this note of grotesque exaggeration gives the poem its peculiar flavour. The final three stanzas of the original poem were poor, including lines like, 'Sergeant, arrest that man who said he winked'. Auden realised that the first two stanzas were the germ of a better poem and in 1936 he turned it into a song when he was collaborating with Benjamin Britten.

The subsequent history and influence of the poem is not mentioned by Fenton but it is just as interesting. It has, in fact, been a model for Fenton himself: 'God: A Poem' uses a similar litany of calculatedly bizarre images. Simon Armitage comes even closer in one of the poems in the 'Book of Matches' sequence: 'Ignite the flares, connect the phones, wind all the clocks;/the sun goes rusty like a medal in its box –/collect it from the loft. Peg out the stars,/replace the bulbs of Jupiter or Mars'.

The only thing that is surprising about the popularity of 'Funeral Blues' is the near-60-year timelag. Despite the wit and clarity of so many of his sonnets and lyrics, Auden's poetry has been regarded as a difficult. Well, some of it is but scattered amongst the *oeuvre* with its complicated history of revisions and deletions is a body of work that is more lucid, more Shakespearean, yet more true to the 20th century than any other poet's. This was the conclusion that Peter Porter came to in his magisterial essay on Auden in last winter's *Poetry Review* ('Poets on Poets', Vol 83 No 4).

Perhaps the problem has been one of packaging? One can imagine a popular *Best of Auden*, but such a book does not exist. The current *Selected Poems*, chosen by Edward Mendelson, is a great improvement on Auden's own selection, but it does not include 'Funeral Blues', 'Tell Me the Truth About Love', or several more of the most accessible sonnets which can be found in *The English Auden*. Then there's 'Through the Looking Glass', and the light-verse masterpiece *Letter to Lord Byron*, available in *The English Auden*, *Collected Poems*, or *Collected Longer Poems*.

Faber have recently been publishing scholarly editions of Auden, the latest of which is the *Libretti and other dramatic writings*, reviewed by Glyn Maxwell in Vol 83 No 4. Edward Mendelson, Auden's literary executor, does a fine job with a canon rendered chaotic by Auden's self-editing. But surely, there is a case for the popular Auden? Faber seem to agree. They have rushed out a booklet of ten of the songs, *Tell Me the Truth About Love*, price £2.50, and in July will publish the paperback *Collected Poems*. For the moment, the best single volume remains the *Collected Shorter Poems*, with the *Collected Poems* nudging it when the paperback is ready. But both these books have serious omissions which at present only *The English Auden* can rectify. Can we have a *Best of Auden*, please?

# The 'Poitry' Man

*John Mortimer on the letters of a poet he admires 'only just this side of idolatry'*

**John Betjeman,**
*Letters Volume I: 1926-1951,*
Ed. Candida Lycett Green,
Methuen, £20
ISBN 0 413 66950 5

Sometime in February 1926 John Betjeman wrote to a lady called Mary St. Claire-Erskine. He told her he has had 'flu, was sorry she'd had 'flu and added that he'd been reading Wells and found him underrated. This letter appears to throw little light on H.G. Wells, not much on the 'flu and nothing on the poems of a writer whom I, for one, admire only just this side of idolatry. What seems extraordinary is that Mary St. Claire-Erskine should have kept it, and that it's survived for some 65 years. Do the Mary St. Claire-Erskines of this world, not to mention the Bogs, Little Prawlies, and Obscurities (Betjeman's pet names for Alan Pryce Jones, Anthony Barnes and Hubert de Cronin Hastings respectively) keep cupboards, lofts, rooms stuffed with correspondence for reproduction in books like this, which is, after all, only the first stout volume of Betjeman letters?

The next question is now much we need to know of the daily lives of the poets. Philip Larkin's letters suddenly, and to the grief of many admirers, revealed him as a racist with the political views of an unreconstructed taxi driver. Although they may have done nothing to add to the appreciation of his verse they gave, at least, a curious and alarming insight into his character. In the opposite way Byron's letters are so good, so entertaining and so endearing that they overshadow his poetry. Betjeman's letters are friendly, gently funny, occasionally over-whimsical, a little arch in his literal spelling of comical and assumed accents, but quite without spite, jealousy, or many real signs of suffering. For deep feelings, and moments of sadness it is necessary to be swept along by the moving tide of Betjeman's verse. The letters are those of a kind and charming man who wrote to please his correspondents and died regretting that he hadn't had enough sex.

The book is interspersed with passages of biography of her father by Candida Lycett Green, who has also edited the letters. These are extremely well written and told me more about Betjeman than the letters themselves. It's in these sections that his daunting and wonderful wife, Penelope, who rode her horse across India, sometimes introduced it into drawing rooms and distressed her husband by her conversion to Rome, comes most fully to life. She was, her daughter writes, a woman who didn't know the meaning of the word embarrassment and always left the door open while going to the lavatory. It's in Candida Lycett Green's account that Betjeman's love for the blonde, full bodied and beautiful Margaret Wintringham also comes alive. She wrote poetry and said she greatly enjoyed washing and ironing Betjeman's handkerchief. Penelope used to call her 'John's Poitry girl' and would take the children out in the pony and trap so that John and Margaret could be left alone to discuss 'Poitry'. Although he wrote that he constantly saw her in his mind's eye – 'I hear your fading voice. I look into your Lincolnshire blue eyes. I think of your curves. Longing springs...' – it's hard to tell if this passion was ever consummated, or if Margaret Wintringham was also a subject of terminal regret.

What emerges from these letters is a portrait of an extremely sensitive soul, of great literary talent, who, almost by way of self protection, invented a comic, appealing and eccentric character for himself which gradually took him over. This is a common occurrence among important writers, the character Byron invented for himself being the most complex and entertaining. Evelyn Waugh conceived a choleric and intolerant old red-faced country squire and became trapped inside his creation. Both John Osborne and Kingsley Amis fancied the guise of crusty old clubmen with reactionary opinions. Even Philip Larkin's racism may have been a kind of theatrical disguise.

John Betjeman's chosen character, the lover of Victorian churches and crumbling seaside resorts, the kindly old gent with occasional spasms of lust, who would feign terror on walks round the garden and speak, over long periods, in an American accent and in the rhythm of 'Hiawatha', the old sweetie who called the lavatory the 'Lavery' after a Victorian painter and called peeing 'standing up', the perpetual schoolboy who, in adult life, sent correspondents drawings of his Teddy Bear dancing, was a far more likeable personality than most adopted by similar talents.

The true Betjeman emerges in his verse. In 1950

he wrote five rules for poetry for the South African poet Patrick Callinan. They are not bad precepts for all poets to remember:

> 1) Poetry should not be private, but easy for all to understand.
> 2) It should have tones of meaning beneath the surface one.
> 3) It should read out loud well.
> 4) It should be memorable.
> 5) It should very clearly not be prose. Rhythm helps to make it different.

It seems to me that these rules are admirably adhered to in his own poetry and much of it has what Housman said was important, the power to raise your hairs when you recall it while shaving. Thinking of Betjeman we should remember that he was able to write like this:

My head is bald, my breath is bad

Unshaven is my chin,
I have not now the joys I had
When I was young in sin.

I run my fingers down your dress
With brandy certain aim
And you respond to my caress
And maybe feel the same...

Too long we let our bodies cling,
We cannot hide disgust
At all the thoughts that in us spring
From this late-flowering lust.

In all its pleasant 500 odd pages there's nothing in the volume of letters to raise the hairs like this.

**John Mortimer's** *Murderers and Other Friends* **will be published by Viking in October; he is currently working on a dramatization of** *A Christmas Carol* **for the RSC.**

## WENDY COPE
## *An Ending*

Don't want to leave this place,
This time, this happiness:
Loud water, muddy tracks,
Trees rooted in pink rocks,
Our lush, steep-sided glen,
Friends I may see again
But certainly not here,
Not in this world we were.

For one short month our home,
This world will soon be gone.
Though those unruly birds
Still chirp and caw, though woods
Breathe on, if we return,
Each one of us alone,
It will not be to find
What we now leave behind.

Out there beyond the gates,
We'll dance on random routes
Through space and time.  How far,
How long, we can't be sure.
We'll have to say goodbye
To more than this one day.
Tomorrow, we rehearse,
And quietly leave this place.

## PETER SCUPHAM
### *Accident*

**I**

Dear reader, I'm writing this to tell you
How a small freckled girl walked by the verge
With a white dog and her grandfather.  Can we take this further?
You are dear to me, my lucky, astonishing friend.
We make rapprochement on the lip of sleep,
And though I shut my eyes, you keep yours open.
We do not read much at night in the blowing libraries,
But now, I like to think, her page lies open,
Slipping its catch between your beings and doings,
Tempting you to a view through its white window.
Here, then is the girl, closed on her own meaning
As she walks from a glimpse to an image.  Now,
She should be eating her dinner. 'Reader' is easy.
If I give you another line, will she be a sonnet?

**II**

But have you taken this in? There could be a problem.
In this line, perhaps one of cadence, that amour de voyage:
A girl and a dog, and her grandfather; yesterday's roadside
Blurred by the tune of a late-Victorian metric.
And how should a line like this hold your span of attention?
How was she dressed? Shall I tell you? How would you dress her?
Oh, fol-de-rols, bright flows of things.  Blue jeans?
Look, you know when you're in the front passenger-seat
And the driver brakes without warning, almost too late,
You swing, weightless and out of your assumptions
With a 'What the hell are you doing?' Well, glance in
The mirror.  What's there? A clumsy line break,
A repeated 'white' in the first section?
What's happened?

**III**

Let's start again.  Were you given this book? Did you buy it?
As yet I can't see its cover, or where it's lying,
Least of all, where I shall be when you read it.
What hubris, trusting us to have this future
In which to make a special sense of nonsense.
Let's get back to the business in my hand
And strip away those qualifiers: white, small, freckled.
Combined, they call to me with a tender disgust
As if I'm talking of a mouse in a laboratory.
And was the man her grandfather? Please forget them.
But though your limbo file is full of adjectives,

Remember the man who kept his treasure safe
By one condition. Whoever dug it up
Must not think of a white badger while he dug for it.

## IV

*I'm telling you the truth.* Because we *share,*
(Each is the Red King in the other's dream),
And each of us has space and time, can spare
A little of ourselves upon this theme,
It is important that we learn to trust,
If not each other, girl and road and man.
Do not believe the useful rhyme of 'dust',
Believe that I can make a sonnet scan.
A neat container: what then is contained?
A stopped frame from a film that's running free,
A coarse and grainy stuff that's not explained
By titling it in bold **'Life', 'Memory',
'Gone with the Wind',** or subbing out the text
With flickering cartouches of 'What comes next'.

## V

For what comes next is something we can make
Only in easy half-light and the half-rhymes:
Bright, broken things, the seductive lilt of the dark
Patting about with words at the old names –
August, with a fly-blown ache of sky,
Smelling of war and slow holiday,
With its Panama hat and a dolly-twist of straw,
Rough pasture, and a half-blind terrier,
A gravelled voice, pacing words slowly
And throat-stopped now for half-a-century,
A brass ferrule poked in a molehill,
The sag of wires from pole to pole
Black with birds and silver with sound,
The held hand lost in the holding hand.

## VI

How can I count her losses as they pass?
I cannot count my own. Each loss must be
Particular and endless. Does the dry grass,
At summer's end, whisper 'Remember me.'
There is a blur of dry and green, a car
Spacing itself to where the day begins –
They're something still, but were not what they are,
Such particles have glimmered from their skins,
Each photon stuck and hinged inside a head,
Probing the space-time of the zodiac

Or lying down, pretending to be dead,
Beyond the spooky half-life of its track –
Reader, what do you see? Let's play 'I-Spy',
Scrambling the skylights of a single eye.

## VII

Let's take a sodden castle, in a rain
Which mizzles blue and unremembered hills.
Stand on the magic carpet.  Count each pane
Of puzzled glass.  The rocky landscape fills
That crazy paving with the ghosts of trees
Which meet the ghosts of chiffoniers and clocks
And offer up their crystal truancies
To light which greets the window, and unlocks
A living space: one bright, and real, and so,
Where loll-tongue dog and man and chattering girl
Can meet in fiction's radio-active glow,
Conspire to make our head and heartaches whirl.
Outside and in don't match.  A missing room
Hides dust and lanthorns, memoires d'outre-tombe.

## VIII

Is it Lot 93, or 92?
The sharp-nosed auctioneer, two lots a minute.
'What am I bid?' No provenance, no signature.
A rural scene.  Amateur, but not a print.
The gangling man in leathers, the holiday-makers
In from the rain, and Mrs Moore, dealer in bric-a-brac,
Are silent.  Everything must belong somewhere,
Be at home in a finite series of numbers.
It's a rotten likeness of something, but still a likeness,
And will grow lovely if you grow to love it:
An old man blurred enough to make an ancestor,
The dog and child whose trust, fidelity,
Is all you feel, and all you feel you've lost,
The frame waving goodbye as they walk towards you.

## IX

There is merriment and puzzle in Cookham Churchyard
At the moment of resurrection, when all discover
The relief of realising they need no adjectives,
Or need them only in the Pickwickian sense,
As nuns own maiden-names, or rosaries.
No-one says 'What a funny hat you're wearing!'
'That walking-stick was Jim's.'  There are no brand-names
For brands plucked from the burning, the saints and martyrs
That we have dignified to be our votive images.
And if the Panama hat, the aertex shirt belong,
They must belong as prayers and flames belong,

Clothing the lost majesty of Proper Names,
Which, at their most proper, become as common
As man and girl, as dog, as road.

**X**
Dear reader, I've written this to tell you . . .
Of this accident, this impact. I drove within my limits.
There was no tyre-squealing; there were no skid-marks.
All that humming cage remained responsive;
Just a catch in the engine's throat, a change in the fine-tuning.
I pulled the car in carefully to the verge
And remembered the hazard-warning indicators.
A bit too late. I realised I'd gone clean through them,
But the sun picked them up in its own good time,
Walking no more, and no less carefully.
I think the girl might have been carrying flowers.
What do you think, dear reader? You're the only one
Who has some cause to make a claim against me.
Is our cover comprehensive? Shall we call it knock for knock?

*Peter Scupham's new collection,* **The Ark,**
*was published by Oxford Poets in June, price £6.99.*

## ALAN DIXON
### *Walking from Allotments*

Was it quite such a cliché once to praise
A work for looking sexy? It seemed right
About the drawings of Jules Pascin showing
The human ways of being without knowing.
His lecherous line and colours could amaze
And had their swift affairs with quenchless white.

I think of them again as I walk home
With bucket and watering can. One more hot day!
Two Caribbeans linger by a shed
Where a bike is propped, their hats the perfect way
For Pascin with impatience to capture them.
The scribbled fence, the cat that trots ahead,
The ragged greens and every useful plant
Disclose themselves, arouse the celebrant.

*Alan Dixon's* **The Hogweed Lass** *is published by Poet & Printer, 30 Grimsdyke
Road, Hatch End, Middlesex HA5 4PW, price £3.00.*

# Love Lies Sleeping

*Lavinia Greenlaw on the letters of a poet with an 'all-embracing enthusiasm for experience' – Elizabeth Bishop*

**Elizabeth Bishop,**
*One Art: The Selected Letters,*
Ed. Robert Giroux,
Chatto & Windus, £25.00 hbk,
ISBN 0 7011 6195 7

Elizabeth Bishop insisted that the way to get to know a poet was to read: 'ALL of somebody. Then read his or her life, and letters ...' This seems the right order in which to go about it – the letters following on from a reading of the work and life. And so Robert Giroux's vast selection, with its comprehensive biographical introduction, complements but also depends upon the *Complete Poems* and *Prose*, and the illuminating work of a critic like David Kalstone (*Becoming a Poet: Elizabeth Bishop with Marianne Moore and Robert Lowell*).

*One Art* includes more than 500 letters written by Bishop between the age of 17 and her death at 67, to more than 50 correspondents. Giroux drew these from the 3,000 that were available to him. Doubtless, there were many more. Bishop was a prolific letter-writer, recording, documenting and compulsively sharing her observations and experiences. She seems to be the kind of person that liked to climb a mountain in silence but who then got great pleasure from having someone with whom to celebrate the view. Bishop bestows anecdotes and observations, as she offers advice on recipes and healthcare. There is serious intent behind her throwaway touch: she is giving with great care, giving something she feels the recipient can not only enjoy but can also use. Aunt Grace in Nova Scotia is offered local Brazilian colour and character in a way that relates to her own village life; for Marianne Moore, the treatment of the same subject is altogether more anthropological. Bishop was conscious of the craft of writing a good letter: 'kind of like working without really doing it'. She even gave a seminar on the art of letterwriting and collected letters by writers such as Coleridge, Hopkins and Woolf. Bishop could not help but take care with her letters although this never interfered with their immediacy which is such that at times they contain a running commentary of household calamities or are left off from for hours or days as she is distracted.

There is an ease of communication in her correspondence which is not apparent in her life. Despite her many devoted friends and supporters, she described herself to Robert Lowell as 'the loneliest person that ever lived'. Perhaps the absence and distance that necessitate letters, made safe certain dangers for Bishop, such as exposure or intimacy. After returning to the States, she confessed 'I almost felt that I understood people, or they me, better in Brazil than now when I'm here on the same continent with them'.

The first letters Giroux includes give an early indication of her all-embracing enthusiasm for experience. At eighteen, in a few paragraphs, she relishes the drama of capsizing a sailing boat, delights in the overwhelming pink of the room in which she is staying, and compliments her friend's essay on *Comus*. This strikingly eclectic list is an early indication of her *aesthetic* use of dramatic contrast. This is not to imply that Bishop concentrated on effects but that she was interested in effects as much as action, in what things did to each other as much as what they did to her.

The delicate, expert balance of objectivity and engagement that characterizes her poetry can be seen in these letters again and again. There is also a willingness to give everything full consideration, countered by the impatient honesty of her response. This is apparent in her careful but head-on criticism of the work of friends such as Lowell and Moore. Her visual response is equally irrepressible as she delights in plants and paintings, or the pleasure of cooking an artichoke.

Bishop's handling of crises in her correspondence reflects her way of dealing with enormities in her work. When she is ready to take control, she is direct, not afraid of big ideas or big language. And yet, beyond plain statement, she does not indulge or impose. She asks that some of her most desperate letters be destroyed. The discomfort with which we read such inclusions extends to the humiliating descriptions of her fight against alcoholism. She struggled with asthma all her life, and a catalogue of other illness and accidents, always seemingly suffering from physical unease or being smothered or overwhelmed. Illness, like alcohol, could be a useful retreat or provide necessary barriers or sub-stance: 'I still have asthma but right now feel it is useful, like sandbags in a balloon'.

These letters do, after all, tell us a great deal about her poetry, starting with her early experiments with form. While she struggled to find her poetic voice, she clearly knew what it was she was after. In 1933, she quotes the Baroque ideal as the convention she would like to follow: 'to portray, not a thought, but a mind thinking ...' This idea is central to her work, showing the cogs turning as perception is formed: 'the city grows down into his open eyes/inverted and distorted. No. I mean/ distorted and revealed,/ if he sees it at all' ('Love Lies Sleeping'). This is acknowledgement of process, not self-consciousness, the dangers of which she understood well.

There is also, of course, all the evidence of the mundane side of the poet's life – submissions, rejection, and the anxiety and depression that so often accompany publication. Also, the familiar mix of certainty and sensitivity: 'I've never minded criticism a bit, strange to say – but what if this reviewer ... says the TRUTH?' Bishop acknowledges her own fragility through admitting the fragility of her peers – 'look at poor Cal – and Marianne, who hangs on just by the skin of her teeth and the most elaborate paranoia I've ever heard of'. The timespan of this selection is also a record of the long gestation of each of her poems and books. On the final poems for *A Cold Spring*, she writes 'I've stalled and stalled about two or three poems for a year almost'. 'The Moose' took her sixteen years. In 1956, she writes to her Aunt Grace that she has begun a long poem about Nova Scotia, to be dedicated to her. It was finished in 1972.

While she eschewed the politics of the poetry world, Bishop counted many poets among her most important correspondents. These included Randall Jarrell, May Swenson and James Merrill, but above all Robert Lowell and Marianne Moore. Introduced to Moore in 1934, Bishop quickly developed a close relationship with her, based on the elder poet's editorial interventions in her work. Only after four years of correspondence was she invited to call Moore by her first name – an event Bishop celebrated with a capitalized MARIANNE drawn as if spelt out in lights. Her first letter to Moore is

formal, respectful and grateful, ending in the incongruous mention of a fascinating new book about tattooing. This conscious collection of exotica for Moore continues throughout the correspondence, as Bishop makes it her duty to describe and collect, to pass experiences on to Moore whom she fails to entice out into the world. This difference between them – Moore's observations of novelty as opposed to Bishop's experience of the new – grew increasingly large, and Bishop, while needing Moore's clear eye and stillness of vision to focus her early work, felt the burden of such clinical observation. In 1935, having dutifully written to Moore from France, she confesses to Frani Blough, 'what a blessing it is ... I don't feel dutybound to ... DESCRIBE everything'. On the other hand, Bishop sometimes uses intense descriptive passages to avoid or change the subject such as in her increasingly awkward exchanges with Moore.

In 1947, Bishop was introduced to Robert Lowell, a meeting he later remembered with misty-eyed nostalgia that in one affectionate and humorous letter, Bishop gently deflates. Despite her apparent lack of sentiment for the occasion, they were vital to each other thereafter. They met infrequently, tongue-tied as poets often are when meeting within each other's families, but never stopped corresponding. Bishop once admitted to him: 'Please never stop writing me letters – they always manage to make me feel like my higher self ... for several days'. The most extraordinary moment in this book comes when Giroux includes a letter from Lowell, written in 1957, confessing that nine years earlier he was on the verge of asking her to marry him. This is the only time Giroux gives us the other side of the conversation and Lowell's letter is overwhelming, insistent and yet accepting: 'asking you is the might-have-been for me, the one towering change, the other life that might have been had'. Bishop waited four months to reply and then ignored this admission completely. Perhaps she perceived his confession to be framed by the exaltation of mania; or maybe she chose a response through which the delicate equilibrium of their intense friendship could survive.

Probably the most important person in her life was Lota de Macedo Soares, with whom she lived for sixteen years in Brazil. Lota provided a secure home but more importantly their relationship seems

> **'The most extraordinary moment in this book comes when Giroux includes a letter from Lowell, written in 1957, confessing that nine years earlier he was on the verge of asking her to marry him.'**

to have been largely a generous one. Her letters of this period are full of passion and continual discovery, of her new country but also implicitly of her new life. Bishop celebrates Lota's character, determination, passion and obsessions. They seem infinitely kind to one another, separate but inseparable, united by individual and mutual passions. It is a great loss that Bishop's letters to Lota were destroyed. Their last few years together were painfully dominated by Lota's involvement in politics, and her increasing ill health. Bishop is loyal, insisting to many of her friends that the difficulties this entails are worth it. Eventually, she faces the impossibility of the situation – the loss of herself which can be traced through a shift from gladly sharing letters with Lota to a plea that the recipient takes care with their response in case they are read by her. Lota's breakdown and eventual suicide overshadow the rest of Bishop's life and are recorded with a characteristic lack of either palliative or adornment.

Returning to the United States, Bishop was forced to overcome her dislike for readings, reviewing and teaching in order to make herself secure, describing herself in 1970 as a 'scared elderly amateur "professor" ...' Strength and helplessness play an equal part in the correspondence of her final years. She is as self-deprecating as ever, comically describing the occasion when her students end up finding her a place to live, and move her in while she goes down town to get her hair done. Similarly, she welcomes but is bewildered by the new America of laundromats and supermarkets. She dislikes California and Reagan in particular but enjoys friendships with new writers such as Denise Levertov and Thom Gunn, and is interested in seeing *Bonnie and Clyde* and *A Clockwork Orange*.

The final letter in this book was written on the day Bishop died. She argues with John Nims about some footnotes he wants to use with her poems. The letter begins 'I'm going to take issue with you rather violently ...' and ends 'Yours Affectionately'. As Bishop once said to Randall Jarrell, 'communication is an undependable but sometimes marvelous thing'.

## VICKI FEAVER
### Bufo Bufo

Clown's name for the creature
in my cellar. I give him gladly

the one room I don't want:
sodden cardboard, wet dark,

the gluey varnish of slugs.
What he eats: dollops

of glassy, yellow-grey meat,
host to scavenging mites –

the only things down here
to move fast. He creeps

over the floor's uneven brick
as if movement is painful,

or crouches still, under the drip
from a leaking pipe, moist

and glistening, pumping
himself to bursting.

It's spring, when toads smell their way
to water, and the females' spawn

is strung in necklaces of black-eyed beads.
But he's my prisoner – soft, warty stone

who at night swells
to the size of a man.

## SOPHIE HANNAH
### *The Only Point is Decimal*

Ninety per cent of places are not worth going.
Ninety per cent of jobs are not worth doing.
Ninety per cent of men are not worth knowing.
Ninety per cent of women are not worth screwing.

    An attitude like yours must take some practice.
    Part apathetic, mostly condescending,
    Lukewarm then spiky, vichyssoise-cum-cactus,
    That's you, my friend.  Or are you just pretending?

Ninety per cent of books are not worth reading.
Ninety per cent of songs are not worth singing.
Ninety per cent of advice is not worth heeding.
Ninety per cent of numbers are not worth ringing.

    Life passes by, but you are not impressed.
    You'd rather be a lonely couch potato
    Than compromise.  There's no point getting dressed
    For anyone less erudite than Plato.

Ninety per cent of chances are not worth taking.
Ninety per cent of corners are not worth turning.
Ninety per cent of hands are not worth shaking,
Ninety per cent of candles are not worth burning.

    And all that I can think is what a shame.
    What are the odds you'll wonder where I went?
    The chances of you knowing why I came?
    Point zero zero zero one per cent.

**Sophie Hannah's first collection will be published by Carcanet next year.**

# Storm Warnings: Adrienne Rich in conversation with Sarah Maguire

Like most poets I go along to readings at the South Bank as much for the social interaction as the poetry. What's fascinating, particularly about the big ones at the Purcell Room, is who is present and who is absent. Book an actual or potential Nobel prize winner and you can't get to the bar for the London-Oxbridge-nexus boys, as well as many of us less exalted creatures. Book Adrienne Rich and not one was in sight. (Not that you could get to the bar this time either as tickets had been sold out for weeks.) But the women were there. Rarely have I seen such a delightful collection of women poets under one roof. Rarely (never?) have I been to a reading when the audience cheered in the Purcell Room. So why is Adrienne Rich so important as a poet – at least if you're a woman writing poetry?

Women poets of my generation are all writing in the wake of Adrienne Rich, consciously or not, simply because she's changed our agenda, extended our paradigms; just as we are all writing in the wake of feminism, whatever our politics; it's the *Zeitgeist* we can't breathe outside. What Adrienne Rich has done for us, particularly in her early essays such as 'When We Dead Awaken: Writing as Re-Vision' published in 1971, is to address the issues of how it is possible to be a woman and a poet without being viewed as exceptional, as a surrogate man. Never before have so many women been writing – and publishing – so much poetry as they are nowadays (just think what it was like merely a decade ago). Of course Adrienne Rich as an individual is hardly responsible for this great social development. But I do think that without her example and her criticism things would have been that bit harder for many of us.

In May she came over to London to promote her new book of essays, *What is Found There: Notebooks on Poetry and Politics*, through an extensive reading tour. We spent two hours talking together, focussing largely on the shifts her poetry has undergone during her long and distinguished career.

In the past forty-five years Adrienne Rich has published fifteen collections of poetry. Throughout, her work has continued to change and develop, each book seeming relevant to its time, each book laying bare the processes of grappling with the formal and ethical issues of its moment. Her first collection, A *Change of World* (1951), was cho-

sen by Auden to be published in the prestigious Yale Younger Poets Series when she was only twenty-one. In his patronizing 'Introduction' to the volume Auden wrote, 'The poems a reader will encounter in this book are neatly and modestly dressed, speak quietly but do not mumble, respect their elders but are not cowed by them, and do not tell fibs; that for a first volume, is a good deal'. Adrienne Rich, in other words, was being a 'good girl'. Nowadays though, a reader of this Cold War book is more likely to be struck by the constrained tension of that book, by the number of poetic 'storm warnings', however quietly spoken, however formally polite. In her essay 'When We Dead Awaken: Writing as Re-Vision' Adrienne Rich wrote, 'In those years formalism was part of the strategy — like asbestos gloves, it allowed me to handle materials I couldn't pick up barehanded'.

Of her second book, *The Diamond Cutters*, Adrienne Rich said, 'It's a very bad book for the most part I think – it feels very derivative to me and like a tremendous effort. A lot of that had to do with this first manuscript being chosen by Auden and published by the Yale University Press. I had no idea what to do with that. It was an identity I couldn't grasp – that of published poet. I thought of myself still as an apprentice poet – and I was – and I should have been. Then at that point I married, and my first child was born when the second book was in proof. This has something to do with both the cautiousness of that book, and the fact that I realised that I had to break out of this formal mode of doing things. Life had gotten really messy and anarchic. Domesticity never seemed safe to me – it seemed very dangerous!'

It took Adrienne Rich eight years to find a way of getting out of the mode of writing which characterizes these first two books – a period in which she gave birth to three sons (in 1955, '57 and '59). As she said, 'When you really aren't getting enough sleep, creativity suffers. However, I did write during those years. I would get up in the middle of the night with a child and write a few lines, so I ended up with all these scraps, and that was what eventually I realised was the long poem called 'Snapshots of a Daughter in Law'. I began to see the possibility that what I had were not just fragments, but that they were the fragments of something bigger. Then finally I remember numbering them, as if they belonged to something larger.

'By then I was reading a lot of poets whom I had not read, or whom I hadn't read attentively before, such as William Carlos Williams. I had met Denise Levertov, which was a very important connection for me to make because she was entirely involved with the Black Mountain poets, with Creeley and Duncan and Olson and others, and she was also a woman, and she was also the mother of a son, in a marriage – and so this was like a tremendous opening up of possibilities for me, I mean just that combination. In a certain way we were both token women in our different poetic geographies but we of course didn't realise that at the time! But we did talk about what it was like to have a child and to try to write.

'Until the book *Snapshots of a Daughter in Law* came out [in 1963] I had been rather a darling of the poetry reviewers and had been doing just nicely; but then there were grumbles and remarks about my having sacrificed beauty, about the jaggedness of the lines, about my abandonment of music. (Although, of course, I don't think I've ever abandoned music – it's a different music, a more complex music. I much prefer the longer line, the looseness of it. I think it's more difficult. You can write iambic pentameters endlessly and, at least in sound, go on repeating yourself. I think that's why people like Williams wanted to smash the iamb: they felt this confinement was deleterious to poetry.) But when *Snapshots* came out, the same critics who had loved me were not so sure – they slapped my wrists and said that I should go back to what I did so beautifully. That was very disconcerting. And what was more disconcerting was they accused me of being political – which I had no idea I was being! And of being at the same time too personal. It was the poem 'Snapshots of a Daughter in Law' that was seen as personal and bitter. I was working in a certain sense unconsciously in that book. I was doing what I felt I had to do. And so I had to go back and think, 'What am I doing here?'

'I think it's notable that, although in a lot of the poems in *Necessities of Life* [published in 1966] I went on doing certain similar things [to the work in *Snapshots*], those poems are much more obliquely personal, and a lot of them are about death. I really was thinking, "I can't go back to what I used to do; if what I'm doing now, and feel I must do, is increasingly going to alienate me as a poet, then what do I have?" I felt very despairing during the time those poems were written.'

I asked Adrienne Rich what her relationship with Robert Lowell was during that time. 'I had

already begun to feel the necessity to write differently, to write a different kind of poem when *Life Studies* came out [in 1959] so the book seemed to me to be further confirmation of that. At the time I had material which was personal, which in no way was I going to put into poems directly in the way that Lowell was putting his own private life into poetry. But the *structure* of some of those poems was what I was able to get a lot from. It was the combination of personal life with the historical sense, that was the thing that was very, very important to me about Lowell.'

I also asked Adrienne Rich about her contact with Sylvia Plath who, for years, secretly regarded Rich as her 'arch-rival', the woman poet whom she most admired – and envied for her talent and success.

'Sylvia was always very nice to me. I didn't have the feeling that she was jealous of me. Of course, at that point everyone saw Ted as The Poet. We all knew that she was writing poetry, but his book *The Hawk in the Rain* had just come out in the States. I must have seen some of her poetry written after she came back here in little magazines or anthologies. But it wasn't until after her death when the posthumous work was published in the States that anyone seemed to have any idea of her significance. It was a shock. I remember Lowell taking me out to lunch and he was armed with this copy of *Encounter* and there was a whole bunch of her posthumous work in there including some of the bee poems – and they were absolutely dazzling.

'I was teaching by then [the mid-'sixties] and I was running into women students who were cultists of Plath who assumed that the poetry drew its energy from the destructive urge. I kept trying to say in this flattening way that when someone has a gift for language like that it can be applied to any kind of experience. The fact that some of these poems seemed to be pointing toward death doesn't mean that they couldn't point in other directions had other things been different. The energy in that poetry is incredible. Sylvia Plath is not a confessional poet. That term has done so much to diminish poetry in a certain way, and to diminish some of the most striking and promising poetry too, because it's like you name it and you kill it – you drive a pin through the butterfly as you name it.

'I'm not crazy about this term postmodernism because it seems to me to mean too many things to too many people at this point (rather like feminism!) but in a way her poetry seem to me to be a kind of post-modern breakthrough. I think that it's very quintessentially a woman's poetry with a lot of female physicality in it. It's unabashedly in a woman's voice. You never feel that she's trying to sound like an honorary man and at the same time it has a kind of impersonality too. Something in the poetry is held.'

Adrienne Rich continued to open out her work formally in *Leaflets* (1969) and *The Will to Change* (1971), the poems 'Shooting Script' and 'Images for Godard' being influenced by the experimentations of the French New Wave film directors such as Cocteau and Godard himself.

'I was really entranced by Godard's films as they were coming out. I'd love to see a lot of them again. It was his interest in language as well as the image. Film seems to me to be tremendously connected to poetry. And of course the time those poems were written was a very tumultuous time. I remember it as a time of such hope and such creativity. We weren't just fighting back, we were creating new institutions. There was a kind of openness for new ways of doing things, new ways of thinking, new ways of producing.'

Her work was beginning to become more explicitly feminist in intention. *Diving Into the Wreck* (1973) was crucial in this respect. In that book the poems largely confront the difficult ties and breakdowns in male/female relationships. After a five-year interval she published perhaps her most famous collection, *The Dream of a Common Language*, in which she writes for the first time as a lesbian feminist. To some readers and writers of poetry this development clearly seemed like a huge shift in sensibility: 'I never thought of it as anything other than a continuation of my life; it never seemed like a break. I was simply continuing to move in directions I'd been moving in for a very long time, before there was a women's movement, before there was any kind of lesbian gathering. Those movements provided a climate in which I could write things I might not have felt able to write otherwise – and also a language. It was an enormous relief to be able to do that: to be able to come out of the closet as a woman. Women seemed to be growing and blossoming at that time. The energy between women at that time was so powerful, whether they were lesbians or not. It was so absorbing. It was like a whole new terrain we were discovering together.'

After *A Wild Patience Has Taken Me This Far* (1981), which largely continued the themes and emphases of *The Dream of a Common Language*, the collections *Your Native Land, Your Life* (1986) and *Time's Power* (1989), as their titles suggest, see Adrienne Rich engaging with the sense of biography and autobiography within the political and histori-

cal contexts of time and place. Of these two books she said:

'They're books of the eighties. They're books of a period which in many ways was so despairing. I was really trying to write against that despair but having internalized some of it. And I had to look outward, outside of my own country in fact, for any kind of hope. I was reading Margaret Randall's translation of the Cuban women poets and I was reading Nicaraguan poets. I went to Nicaragua briefly and I began to feel a kind of energy out there which I felt was draining away, was leaking out of American life – which wasn't true, but it felt that way. With Reagan you felt the accelerated erosion of the whole social compact. Then there was the ruination of the language – the way it was being twisted and distorted, the way Reagan was able to call the Contras 'freedom fighters' - it was abominable. The intellectual Right were really very consciously seizing the ethically and morally tinged language that the Left had used and turning it around. There are some poems in those books which I feel are strong as poems but it was almost like trying to find the poetic means for the next stage.

'I'm writing poetry again at the moment. I wrote *An Atlas of the Difficult World* [1991] within the years that I was writing *Notebooks* – those books relate to each other. In the last year and a half I really wasn't writing much poetry at all because of finishing up with *Notebooks*...I can never give myself deadlines. I never understand painters who have an exhibition and they paint night and day – how do they do that? But there are times when I have to write. When I'm able to I write every day in some form. When I'm alone in the house – my partner teaches in Connecticut so we're separated from mid-January to mid-May – although I miss her, I'm very good at being on my own. And when she's home I can also do that because she's a writer as well so she understands those needs. I don't know what this next book will look like, but I feel as though a lot of it is Cassandra-like.' In Greek legend, of course, Cassandra's prophecies of doom are both fated to be correct and fated to be ignored. Adrienne Rich's forthcoming storm warnings are something to which we had better pay heed.

**Adrienne Rich's *What is Found There: Notebooks on Poetry and Politics* is published by Norton, price £14,95, ISBN 0 393 03565 4. She has just won a $374,000 (£250,000) MacArthur Fellowship. Sarah Maguire was one of the 20 New Generation Poets.**

# Grump and Grind

*Michael Hulse tries to separate Kipling's poetical wheat from the political chaff*

**Peter Keating,**
*Kipling the Poet,*
Secker & Warburg,
£25.00, ISBN 0 436 23249 9.
**Ann Parry,**
*The Poetry of Rudyard Kipling,*
Open University Press,
£12.99, ISBN 0 335 09494 5.
Rudyard Kipling
***Selected Poems,***
edited by Peter Keating,
Penguin, £5.99,
ISBN 0 14 018477 5.

**M**y earliest memory of Kipling, though of course I didn't know his name, is of my father (not a singing man) singing 'Mandalay'. It was a good tune, but I remember that what I particularly loved, at the age of four or thereabouts, were the flyin'-fishes playing and the dawn coming up like thunder. A few years later, not far into the TV era that began in our home when I was eight, he read 'Danny Deever' aloud, and it must have been about the same time as he read out Goethe's 'Erlkönig' because both poems reduced me to tears and have been associated in my mind ever since. Even later, I learnt to forget that Kipling had ever touched me so directly, and came to despise him for being an imperialist nasty. Does this sound familiar? I have the impression that most readers these days (except for those who give Kipling unqualified approval and read him for the confirmation he can give to unreflecting chauvinism) pass through these stages. In due course I began the business of trying to sort out what appealed to me in Kipling and what I couldn't even begin to like, and of understanding the relation between the two. This is the difficult thing, and it's rare to find a critic who's much help with it.

Peter Keating's basic position is that Kipling was a sodding good poet who has been simplistically misunderstood, while Ann Parry's is that he was the preeminent example of a popular political poet. Keating's stress is on the poetry, and he is especially good at bringing out Kipling's debts to Bret Harte (the opening of 'Mandalay', forsooth), Swinburne, Browning and Burns; the differences as well as the affinities that appear when Kipling's poetry is compared with music hall lyrics; and the nature of Kipling's differences with literary movements that had salon respectability – Nineties aestheticism, and its modification in what we've come to call Modernism. He is very good too on Kipling's ability to choose his own ground, and (for example) gives a masterly account of Kipling's refusal to endorse C.R.L. Fletcher's more extreme prejudices when he supplied verses for Fletcher's mythologizing history of England. Keating's book sets out to place the poetry in the life, so readers of Charles Carrington's standard biography are likely to feel they've been told nothing new – but it's a decent read.

Ann Parry can be ungrammatical one moment and the next will say 'the signifier is over-determined and moveable', but most alarmingly, given her subject, she isn't much good on the poetry at all. She doesn't seem to know what makes it poetry (and tends to misquote it), and the only time in her entire book that she even attempts metrical analysis she gets it revealingly wrong. Glossing these two lines from 'Danny Deever' –

> For they're done with Danny Deever, you can
> 'ear the quick-step play,
> The Regiment's in column, an' they're
> marchin' us away;

– Ann Parry writes: 'The tripping anapaests here suggest a march and contrast with the grave iambics of the previous stanza'. The trouble with this is that the couplet quoted is in fact in the seven-foot iambic line Kipling so frequently used. He's added an extra unstressed syllable at the head of the first line ('For'), substituting an anapaest for that one foot to provide a kickstart lilt; and he's also defeated Parry's ear by his habit of placing a mid-line caesura after an unstressed syllable (after 'Deever' and after 'column') and following the caesura with a syllable that ought to carry a stress but in fact has minimal stress ('you', 'an''), a trick that gives the effect of a repeated kickstart but doesn't by any means remove the lines from their iambic pattern. Parry's inability to cope with even this straightforward kind of substitution suggests that her technical resources aren't up to much, and helps explain why she's so poor on the poetry as poetry. The strength of her book, a real one, lies in her broad and well-marshalled use of historical material to provide a context in which to read Kipling's political views: on this she is better, and has more bite, than Keating.

Both Keating and Parry left me feeling I'd been told little that affected my sense of the poems, and I imagine most readers will prefer to look at the poems themselves. Keating's new Penguin selection is a thinner and weaker choice than Eliot's Faber selection, and by excluding some of the poems that are central to an understanding of Kipling – 'A Song of the English', 'Et Dona Ferentes' 'Fuzzy-Wuzzy' and, staggeringly, 'The Ballad of East and West' – it creates an oddly skewed image of his work. I think the main fact of the poetry, from which all the others follow, is that, where love is the crux for most of us, for Kipling it was power. He seems to have had little real notion of what makes a civilization more than just a heap of people getting and spending and fighting. Of course there are those wonderful moments (mainly in the prose) when Kipling defies simplistic readings – stories such as 'Lispeth', passages in *Kim* – but, despite individual affections, he believed utterly that God 'hath smote for us a pathway to the ends

of all the Earth'. The problem with the men who were running the Empire, to Kipling's mind, was that they weren't tough enough: to defend 'the Glory of the Garden', Kipling and the radical right wanted universal conscription, powerful leadership, and a social system that trained young men to play 'the game' of Empire. It sounds like boy scouts when Kipling urges that their skills be won 'after trial and labour, by temperance, living chaste', but the attitude is of a piece with his pro-Hitlerian insistence that Bolshevism was a Jewish plot, and so forth. Such views, like it or not, aren't separable from the poetry. 'McAndrew's Hymn' and 'Danny Deever', the fine 'Epitaphs of the War', and one or two more, will always deserve their readers, but the difficulty with Kipling's grump and grind will remain that his contempt for democracy, his racial superiority complex, and his love of power and strength, lead directly to his bully-boy metrics, to his patronizing appropriation of anything he thought would please the crowd, and to the lordly disdain he affected when at times he didn't please it. I don't forget that I cried for Danny Deever. But there's more to Kipling than that.

## DAVID SUTTON
### *The Lame Ant*

I have known those who were kindly, not because
They had anything to gain, or thought they had,
Not even, it seemed, from a consciousness of virtue
Or principle of faith; one might have said
Such was their way, from an overflow of gladness
Or because the innocent heart keeps open house
Scorning defence, but anyway, so it was.

I have thought of fairy-stories: how they teach us,
Against all reason, that kindnesses return,
That when the king's son seeks the giant's daughter
What wins the quest is the irrelevant rescue
Of certain wayside ants, who later come
To do the task that he cannot, and gather
The seed the giant has scattered, each last grain.

And I have wondered what part I might play in this,
Knowing myself a grown man, middling hard,
Watchful of my defences, a dour accountant,
Weighing and balancing. And I have thought
That if nothing else I could be one of those
That gather and give back: the lame ant, maybe,
Who brings the last seed in before the nightfall.

# Hardy Country

*Helen Dunmore on a nineteenth-century novelist and twentieth-century poet*

**Martin Seymour-Smith,**
*Hardy,*
Bloomsbury
£25.00  ISBN 0 7475 1037

I drove home through Dorset a couple of weeks ago and saw two scenes which had that bright flash of permanence things possess when seen from a car. They might be going on still, much as Jude is always looking towards Oxford, or Tess lying on the grass at night looking straight up at 'some big bright star'. First there was a pair of skewbalds grazing a wide verge. They were hobbled, but beside them a man was hammering in the post to which they would soon be tethered. Two other men watched him closely as they lounged with their thumbs in their jeans pockets. They were all bare-chested in the warm afternoon sun, while blue smoke flapped up in sheets from the fire by their van. The men were young, dark, sinewy, encamped a little way outside the village. Further on two more men whose hair was the same colour as the pale straw with which they were thatching sat astride a cottage roof, while a third looked up from the ground, talking to them. The thatching was half-done and the innards of the job showed, while bundles of straw lay about on the grass.

These days tourist boards signpost us to 'Heriot Country' and 'Doone Country'. Theme-park Britain is as happy to use literary markers as any others. And yet this miasma of artifice and packaged experience can overlay a real thing, like the Wessex Hardy created as much as he defined it. The truism is that Hardy's Wessex has ceased to exist. Egdon Heath has shrunk to a handkerchief of land; the milking is done by sterilized machinery rather than by warm, breathing Tess and her companions; Stonehenge is surrounded by barriers and there are no more public hangings. But Hardy is not a theme-park writer, and what he wrote about has not disappeared any more than Hamlet's soliloquies have become outdated because our society does not, on the whole, credit the real existence of ghosts.

Martin Seymour-Smith's great assets as a biographer are his thorough respect for his subject, and his sympathetic understanding of Hardy's work. These are not qualities which can be taken for granted in any biographer, and since the first re-views of his novels Hardy has suffered as much condescension as any other major writer. Hardy did not go to university, nor had he a literary family background. These facts gave consolation to contemporary reviewers who possessed these prerequisites for a literary career, but were not able to do very much with them. So insistent was the focus on Hardy's obscure peasant origin and supposed lack of education that many commentators ignored, or were incapable of perceiving, the subtle artistry in his work. Seymour-Smith argues that even literary figures who supported Hardy, such as Leslie Stephen (Virginia Woolf's father) were to some extent blinded by their own presumptions about the capabilities of a writer who was born in a cottage in rural Dorset. Some of this snobbery, Seymour-Smith believes, still colours our view of Hardy and his work, and prevents us from fully appreciating its originality, modernity and sheer extraordinariness. Like Shakespeare, Hardy is thought to have had 'small Latin and less Greek'. Seymour-Smith examines Hardy's early education and lifelong reading with care, and suggests that he was in fact more widely read than Leslie Stephen. It is part of his argument that Hardy was in no sense an untaught, intuitive writer who did not fully understand what he was doing – although, of course, ravishingly gifted when he got things right. Instead he suggests that Hardy was a masterly ironist, a deliberate artist and highly self-aware.

Seymour-Smith sets Hardy carefully in his historical context. He was born when Lord Melbourne was Prime Minister: the same Melbourne who refused to receive a petition against the deportation of the Tolpuddle Martyrs, signed by a quarter of a million people. As a young draughtsman in London Hardy heard Dickens read. He never forgot the public hanging of a woman which he saw in his youth, and yet he lived to write poems in response to the First World War, and on past the year of the General Strike. If Hardy was sometimes fatalistic, it was a fatalism grounded in experience and the history he lived through as well as in his personality. Such a close weaving of history and personal experience is useful in any biography, and in Hardy's case it is illuminating, since the dramatic action of his novels often springs from a tension between individual desires and the mould into which society wishes these to be forced. Sometimes the tension is as slight as a chafing; in the case of Jude or Tess, it leads to tragedy. Seymour-Smith shows with what skill and brilliance Hardy played off historical change against the fortunes of his characters.

There is so much material in Hardy's life that even a biography over 850 pages long will contain gaps. Seymour-Smith's attitude to other Hardy biographers is combative, and Robert Gittings is often in his sights. There's an entertaining subtext to this book in which Hardy comes close to being the bone pulled about by two dogs. When it comes to Hardy's poetry, their approach is so different that it becomes complementary. Seymour-Smith is very good at teasing out undercurrents of thought, and relating them to contemporary ideas and philosophy as well as to Hardy's own inner life. His analysis of the difficult poem 'In Front of the Landscape', which relates it to Nietzsche, is really informative. Seymour-Smith seems able to penetrate Hardy's thought with a blend of intuition and careful research. But Gittings has perhaps a better understanding of Hardy's poetic technique, and his comments on rhythm in Poems of 1912 - 1913 make very good points about Hardy's use of folk-tune: for example, his mimicry of 'a fiddler, double-stopping to indicate the approaching finish of the dance'. I would have liked Seymour-Smith to write more fully on these crucial and beautiful poems, where Hardy looks back past the long course of his first marriage to the early days of his love for his wife Emma, and explores the tragedy of how that love was overlaid. However, Seymour-Smith analyzes both of Hardy's marriages with persuasive skill and without the overconfidence which Gittings shows when writing about what Hardy felt for the women in his life.

This biography stresses the modernity of Hardy's thought, and the intense struggle he had to express it in fiction and poetry in a time when as perfect as possible a concealment of sexual behaviour was equated with morality. Hardy had to write his novels twice: once for serial publication in family magazines, which required considerable bowdlerization (the notorious substitution of a wheelbarrow for Angel Clare's arms as a method of carrying Tess and her companions over a large puddle is just one of the grosser examples of this) and again for book publication. A high point in Hardy's inflammation of public opinion was his challenging assertion that Tess, a fallen woman suitable for lachrymose and moralistic treatment in Victorian fiction, was in fact 'a pure woman'. As he wrote to a friend, 'the parochial British understanding knocks itself against this word like a humblebee against a wall, not seeing that paradoxical morality may have a very great deal to say for itself, especially in a work of fiction'. It is clear throughout the biography that poetry was in a sense Hardy's native language. It was a language he never stopped speaking, though in fiction he became silent – or was silenced – after *The Well-Beloved* in 1897. He had close to thirty years of poetry left in him.

Seymour-Smith presents Hardy to us as a huge figure who has thrown his shadow before him in ways which we are still learning to appreciate. He gave these words to a woman character in 1873: 'It is difficult for a woman to define her feelings in language which is chiefly made by men to express theirs' (Elfride Swancourt in *A Pair of Blue Eyes*). Like Elfride, Hardy came fresh to language from a background which was not clogged by literary conventions. Few writers can have made language more plastic, more adapted to his purposes or more remarkable than he did. This very readable, detailed and passionately-felt biography gives Hardy his due.

**Helen Dunmore's new collection is *Recovering a Body* (Bloodaxe, £6.95).**

## GEORGE SZIRTES
### *Elegy for a Blind Woman*

I

The house beautiful was no longer beautiful
yet high pink walls and recessed panels were gentle
and the lift was an old woman who would forget
where she was, and dark incidental

figures on landings hesitate in the sun
before doorways and kitchens with pans and bare
pipes that snaked free of walls before passing on
behind ornamental railing, down into the stair.

If there were children in apartments below
or above hers they were like pigeons that roosted
briefly on balconies.  One wouldn't quite know
when they had arrived but would find them clustered

then flown, or hear – not exactly their voices –
 but pittering feet and small beaks.  They were
really children and elsewhere, with tangible faces
in a world quite real though invisible to her.


**II**

Unobserved, unadmonished, the china boy
embracing the china girl's ankles was daring,
while she, for her part, pretended not to enjoy
his attention though one could see by what she was wearing

that she was made for it.  Her mother's eyes
stared piteously down at all she could not see:
letters on the cupboard, spoons on tables, dead flies
on windowsills, her hand on her own knee,

and two dead husbands, visible in her head,
the last one kindly, with large yellow teeth,
a bald, rubber-lipped darling of a man.  Instead
the cassette player with its stories, the death

of time, the tapping about in the kitchen, the loud
coarse voice she discovered in her throat and the panic
at any small loss.  She moved through a hostile crowd
of animate objects, in a darkness thick

with temper.  Even her friends were impossible,
and her stethoscope fingers trembled with fury
for moments on end.  Their obtuseness, the trouble
they caused not realising her injury,

whole seconds wasted looking for words, and the kind
woman smiling piteously down, also infuriating
because unseeable, like furniture in the mind
which mind keeps moving about, disorientating.

**III**

She was never lovely, but once as a child
she was sent to a lycée and she returned plump,
delicious, mature, speaking fluent French,
and there was something about her skin and clear eyes

which was perhaps lovely. Later her pebble glasses
misted at weddings, froze in brutal February ice
and there never were children. The greyness set in
as everywhere in the country, with fevers, opiates,

thin chalets on the hill, a uniform dereliction.
Behind the screen children did not touch
her dangling hand, let alone kiss it. Grey
turned to black or whatever colour she called it,

red sunlight, lilac cold, sepia tablecloth.
Her brother came, glistened, fidgeted, died
like the ancien regime which seemed now almost
benevolent, rubber faced, like an ugly child

in a house without fabulous statues or butlers,
where the sun would hesitate on the landing,
clear its throat and pass on, out of the yard,
across the green park, heading for the river.

# César Vallejo: The Great Cholo

### John Hartley Williams on a poet who offers an antidote to literalism

Pablo Neruda described him thus: the great halfbreed. Perhaps there was an element of superciliousness in that. Certainly, Vallejo's poetic personality is very different from the flamboyant gesturalism of Neruda. The Indian element in him, Inca or Quechua, is a strong presence in the writing, the patient, stoical, half-abstracted personality of someone who lives through his fate barefooted.

We are told Vallejo is 'difficult' and maybe he is. To literalism, however, Vallejo offers an antidote. His poems are in the language of the mind's hidden suffering. Without biographical dismay, they release this suffering into language using an imagery that owes nothing to conventional ideas of 'likeness'. Reverdy's idea was that the greater distance a spark has to jump in a metaphor, the truer the image's power. Surrealism perhaps? I don't know where surrealism came from. Maybe it started with Dante, maybe with Lautréamont. It seems to be a Latin invention, and I suspect that the source of its power is an oppositional closeness to the language of ritual and religion. (Vallejo's language is suffused with an heretical glee, Christianity's side is fairly gashed open on the spear of his poems.) English, by contrast, has become an artefact of use, devised to expedite business transactions, scientific explanations. There have been concerted attempts to take away its magical power (the New English Bible and so forth). Vallejo's poetry offers us a kind of intuitive foreignness to set against the goals of an English poetry which is 'objective', 'moral' and 'learned' (particularly in the literary domain). But then I have never been persuaded that Anglicans really believe the wine is actually the blood of Christ.

Vallejo was the youngest of eleven children, born in Santiago de Chuco, Peru, on March 16, 1892. His grandmothers were Chimu Indians, and both of his grandfathers were Spanish Catholic priests. That line of descent is revealed in a photograph of him, which shows a slender, dapperly-suited man, seated on a low wall, snake-head of handkerchief twisting up from breast pocket, Panama-style hat balanced on one knee. He looks about forty years old in the photograph. One hand is on a walking stick, an outsize ring on one finger. He rests his chin in the fist of his other hand, a slight frown on his face, black hair swept back from a cliff-like forehead, high ridge of cheekbones prominent, a deep furrow curving down with the sweep of nostril. A rather feminine mouth. He stares off to the left of the photographer, in sympathy with his own thoughts, which are elsewhere.

He studied at the University of Trujillo and wrote a thesis on 'Romanticism in Castilian Poetry'. His first book was *Los Heraldos Negros* (The Black Messengers), which seems to have been received with incomprehension. In these first poems, the themes of family and sexual love come to the fore and are in some way related to suffering. The 'femininity' of Catholicism seems to play a part in this: hospitality as a female idea, opening home heart (body) to the stranger: 'Beloved, this night you crucified yourself/Upon the curved logs of my lips ...' And again, on the same theme, from a poem called 'Capitulation':

Last night the April grain surrendered
Before the weaponless Mays of my youth ...
She grew thoughtful, garnet and heavy-eyed.
I left at dawn. And from that combat
By night two enslaved serpents entered my life.

*Trilce*, Vallejo's second book, was written when he was in prison (an affray? a misunderstanding? – at any rate, someone got killed). Another characteristic of Vallejo's work is a kind of homeliness. He is a writer intensely preoccupied with the idea of the family:

I now have lunched alone, I have had
No mother or 'please' or 'help yourself' or
                           water
Or father who, over the eloquent offertory
Of green corn ears, by his statue-slowness
Asks for the greater hooks of sound.

That is Vallejo's father, his statue-slowness. When the father, before eating, 'asks for the greater hooks of sound', the image sets up a shivering of tuning forks of response to things that are distant. Images of the father, the son, the mother, echo through all these poems.

Vallejo left Peru on his release from prison and never returned. He arrived in Paris, with nothing but a handbook of French in ten easy lessons. It is recorded that he acquired a girlfriend named Henrietta, who worked and helped to support him. Their diet was potatoes, and when they had cheese as well, they considered it a fiesta. If Vallejo had no lodgings, he slept in parks and in the Paris Metro. He developed elaborate theories. He avoided sitting down in order to prevent his clothes wearing out. He could explain how to step from train to platform in just such a way as to spare shoe leather. In those years, from his arrival in Paris in 1923, through marriage in 1929, to his death in 1938, Vallejo's life was marked by hunger:

I emerge from between my own teeth, sniffing,
Crying out, pushing,
Dropping my trousers ...
My stomach empty, my guts empty,
Poverty pulls me out from between my own
                           teeth,
Caught on a sliver by the cuff of my shirt.

In his notebook he wrote: 'I want my life to fall equally upon each and every one of the units (44 kilos) of my weight' ... 'My metre measures two metres; my kilo weighs a ton'. A late poem, published posthumously, with the ironical title: 'I Am Going To Speak Of Hope' begins: 'I do not suffer this sorrow as César Vallejo. I am not in pain now as an artist, as a man or as a mere living being either. I do not suffer from this sorrow as Catholic, Mohammedan or atheist. Today I merely suffer. If I were not called César Vallejo, I would still suffer from this same sorrow. If I were not an artist I would still suffer from it. If I were not a man or a living being I would still suffer from it. If I were not a Catholic, atheist or Mohammedan, I would still suffer from it. Today I suffer further down. I merely suffer'. This drains suffering of all subjectivity. Suffering does not even depend on being a living man. There is something abysmally comic about this, a hyperbole of regression. *Where has this sorrow come from, all by itself?*

Vallejo's poems seem to act out a sorrowful search for the truth of home. A search which happens as it is written, without 'reflection' in the normal literary sense, without 'morality' or 'narrative'. It is the process of experience itself. The evidence suggests that Vallejo did not find himself in his poems. 'It's strange: I thought that that man was me. He looks exactly like me. So much so that when I turned my head, I was almost sure that he was me and I almost crashed into myself.'

Brown skinned, yet wearing shoes. Neither Spanish nor Indian. An orphan, in some imaginative sense, certainly an exile, Vallejo had definitely planned to return to Peru, but delayed for some reason. He contracted a high fever, of undiagnosable cause, and for several months his temperature wavered between 104 and 106. He died on April 15th 1938.

**The translations used here are from H.R. Hays, *César Vallejo, Selected Poems* (Sachem Press, New York), which is an excellent introduction. Other good translations are to be found in Charles Tomlinson's book *Translations* (OUP), and Clayton Eshleman has translated the posthumous work with Jose Rubía Barcía (University of California, 1978). There is a good selection from Vallejo in Eshleman's *Conductors of the Pit* (Paragon House, New York).**

## JOSÉ HIERRO
### *The House*

This house isn't what it was.
In it, before, there were
Lizards, jugs, hedgehogs,
Painters, clouds and honeysuckles,
Folded waves, poppies,
Bonfire smoke . . .

         This house
Isn't what it was: the sound box
Of a guitar.  Fibromas, futures,
Pasts, distances,
Were never mentioned.
Nobody ever plucked the grave
Accent's bass string: 'We love each other,
I love you, you me, they us . . .'
We couldn't be solemn,
For what, then, would the cat've
Thought, the turtle with his green
Suit, the white mouse,
The acromegalic sunflower . . .

This house isn't what it was.
It's started to walk, step by step,
Slowly deserting us in no hurry.
If it had blazed in pomp, all of us
Would've run to save our skins.
But this way it gives us time for all:
To collect things we now
Realize didn't exist;
To say good-bye politely;
To scour indifferently
The coughing walls where
Oleander cast its shadow,
Shadow and ash of days.

This house was first
Grounded on a beach.  Later,
It set sail for deeper blues.
The crew sang.
Against it, hours
And gales could do nothing.
Yet now it dissolves like
A lump of sugar in water.

What'll the feudal cat do
When learning he has no soul;
And the garlics, what'll
They think on Sunday,
The cask of marc brandy,
Thyme and red lavender, when
They look in the mirror and see
Their faces covered with wrinkles.
What'll they think when they know
They're forgotten by those
Who were proof of their youth,
Their eternity's sign,
Death's lightning rod.

This house isn't what it was.
In the night, by it, mercifully
We continue to be cradled.

**(Translated from the Spanish by Louis Bourne. José Hierro was born in 1922; he and Blas de Otero are the two most representative poets of the first post-Spanish-Civil-War generation.)**

## PETER REDGROVE
### Black Bones

That is a human skeleton under the cataract,
The jet bones shining in the white noise,
The black bones of a man of light;

It is a cascade that accepts
Human form from the bones
That have walked into it, and stand;

It must have been his method of death
To walk into a waterfall and be washed away,
Licked clean down to the jetting bones;

And the bones articulate the roar
Of the cataract that seems to speak
Out of the ribs and skull:

His white-haired sermon from the pelting brow,
The unfathomable water-lidded sockets;
Clad in robes that are foam-opulent,

And never the same clothes twice.

## MAURICE RUTHERFORD
### *The Autumn Outings*

That autumn, I was quick getting away:
    only about
one-twenty on the rain-drenched Wednesday
I locked the premises and motored out,
all staff sent home, all workshop plant closed down,
all sense of any kind of business gone,
and not until I'd driven fifteen miles
along fast-flooding roads back into town,
past rival complexes just clinging on,
did rain let up and vision clear: those files

I'd never see again; that desk, the phone
    that shrilled all day
when first it was installed; not hear the moan
compressors made, be soothed by lathes, nor say
'Good morning George, alright?', or 'Nice one, Bert',
the human touch, no more, not to distract
them too long from their work, but just enough
to let them see I cared, and not to hurt
old feelings as I tried to breast the fact
of cancelled orders, creditors turned rough.

The friendly bank soon bared its teeth – drew blood;
    and then that bane,
the Tax Man, claimed his pound.  And so, the flood.
(Fine detail dims again as, too, the pain
recedes three autumns on; yet loss stays true.)
The rain comes vicious now – wipers full speed,
dipped headlights on, rear fogs – the journey seems
to lengthen every time I live it through,
involuntarily, as when the need
for sleep is scuppered by recurring dreams.

My crowd was breast-fed clichés, meal on meal:
    to pull its weight,
nose to the grindstone, shoulder to the wheel,
and, once it stepped inside the factory gate,
was wedded to its work; slapped all the time
by Newbolt's hand: *Play up, and play the game.*
Well, this sounds fine; but what about the bloke
who's anorexic, short-nosed, cannot climb
to reach the wheel, and never makes the team?
For him such wedding tales are guffs of smoke.

Again the morning paper hits the floor —
    banner headlined:
PIT CLOSURES SHOCK — and umpteen thousand more
are facing broken marriages to mines.
A few, lured by that bit-of-fresh, fool's gold,
pin hopes on boarding-houses, market stalls;
one man sits out his protest down the pit,
while lefties call for strikes with all the old
clenched-fist salutes, and aerosol the walls:
SCARGILL FOR KING and TARZAN IS A SHIT.

Their first few days of idleness will see
    in those it hits
undreamt-of traits in personality:
some will get by and others go to bits;
the strong become the weak, the weak make good
as quickly as it's said.  Then, as the days
stack up to months or, as in my case, years,
high principles get trampled in the mud
where guile and self-survival point new ways
to quick back-pocket jobs, fiddles, and fears

of being caught.  But fears will yield, in time,
    a sort of pride,
though not the social pride that saw men climb
from old-world swamps: a sense that one's defied
the odds, the system; finger-licked the crème,
nose-thumbed some top brass, bested those who made
the rules and all the running.  What survives?
Of Us: too early yet to tell.  Of Them:
'Indifferents and Incapables'; their trade
in UB40s and P45s.

In brass-lined boardrooms up and down the land
    deep in regret
a million more redundancies get planned,
while chairmen's hiked-up salaries are set,
and Urban Councils chase arrears in rents.
Wideboys, insider-dealers, some M.P.s
grow richer by a second home in Spain,
a custom-plated white Mercedes-Benz,
that new portfolio.  True-blue disease.
The spores of loss, somewhere becoming gain.

**Maurice Rutherford's new collection, Love is a Four-letter World, _is due from Peterloo in September._**

# A Fountain Sealed

### Jan Marsh celebrates Christina Rossetti in her centenary year

At the age of 23, Christina Rossetti sent a selection of her poems to *Blackwood's*, the premier periodical of the day, with a letter such as young writers are apt to compose. 'Sir', she wrote,

I am not unaware that the editor of a magazine looks with dread and contempt upon the offerings of a nameless rhymester, and that the feeling is in nineteen cases out of twenty a just and salutary one. It is certainly not for me to affirm that I am the one-twentieth in question, but I hope I shall not be misunderstood as guilty of egotism or foolish vanity when I say that ... poetry is with me, not a mechanism, but an impulse and a reality, and that I know my aims in writing to be pure, and directed to what is true and right.

She also requested an opinion as well as a decision, saying that it was mortifying to have done something sincerely, offer it in good faith, and be ignored. Young poets everywhere will recognize the feeling.

In fact, she was being strategically modest as well as assertive, for she was not really a 'nameless rhymester'. At the age of 17 she had two poems accepted by the weekly *Athenaeum*, and in 1850 she was a major contributor to the *Germ*, the short-lived but renowned magazine of the Pre-Raphaelite Brotherhood, founded by her brothers and their friends. She thus had a respectable beginner's provenance, and the ambition to match her aim of writing 'what is true and right'.

Christina Rossetti's current reputation is that of a pious and melancholy recluse, writing pious and melancholy poetry that occasionally flowered into exquisite lyricism, but was more often warped by religious self-denial and abasement:

Give me the lowest place: or if for me
That lowest place too high, make one more
        low
Where I may sit and see
My God and love Thee so.

'If I were bringing the case against God, she is the first witness I should call', observed Virginia Woolf after reading Rossetti's Collected Works.

Religion certainly occupies a key role in Rossetti's work – just as it does in that of Donne, or Hopkins, or T.S. Eliot. And in many ways her wrestlings with faith and despair are comparable to 'Batter my heart' or 'No worst, there is none'. 'You scratch my surface with your pin', she wrote of the secular world: 'Nay pierce, nay probe, nay dig within,/Probe my quick core and sound my depth ...//Your vessels are by much too strait:/Were I to pour, you could not hold –/Bear with me: I must bear to wait,/A fountain sealed through heat and cold'.

'A fountain sealed' was a favourite self-image, from the *Song of Solomon* 'A garden enclosed is my sister, my spouse; a spring shut up, a fountain sealed'. But the poetry flowed, in over a thousand lyrics and ballads, sonnets, odes, narratives and nursery rhymes. To all intents and purposes Christina Rossetti was a professional poet, measuring herself against the giants. And as Isobel Armstrong has recently remarked in 'Re-reading Victorian Poetry', 'in the depth and range of their projects, and in the beauty and boldness of their experiments with language, Tennyson, Browning and Christina Rossetti stand pre-eminent'.

Her difficulties in getting published in the mid-1850s – the 'many rebuffs' and rejections she received – led her to contemplate other careers. She applied unsuccessfully to nurse in the Crimea, reluctantly undertook 'miscellaneous governessing' and worked for five years at a reformatory for young prostitutes in Highgate. But these did not deflect her from her true vocation: poetry was indeed her main 'impulse and reality'.

She came from a literary family. Her father Gabriele Rossetti, Italian patriot in exile, was a poet and *improvisatore*, from whom she acquired a cradle knowledge of metre and melody in the neo-classic mode. Her achievement was to break this mould, while retaining all its musicality. Ruskin, notoriously, condemned the 'irregular measure' of 'Goblin Market', but everyone else responded to its rhythms. Publisher Alexander Macmillan read the poem to his evening class of working men. 'They seemed at first to wonder whether I was making fun of them', he reported; 'by degrees they got as still as death, and when I finished there was a tremendous burst of applause, I wish Miss Rossetti could have heard it'.

Critics are still finding new things to say about the goblins' erotic merchandise, which is so tempting to Laura:

'Buy from us with a golden curl'.
She clipped a precious golden lock,
She dropped a tear more rare than pearl,
Then sucked their fruit-globes fair or red.
Sweeter than honey from the rock,
Stronger than man-rejoicing wine,
Clearer than water flowed that juice;
She never tasted such before,
How should it cloy with length of use?
She sucked and sucked and sucked the more
Fruits which that unknown orchard bore;
She sucked until her lips were sore ...

The success of her first collection, *Goblin Market and Other Poems*, in 1862 was all the sweeter for coming so late (relatively speaking: she was 31). But the rejections were a disguised blessing; early acclaim is often an enemy of promise, and much of Rossetti's best work was produced when she was writing without great hopes of publication. Once *Goblin Market* had made her name, she was under continual pressure to publish. When would her second collection be ready? Macmillan inquired. Had she more pieces for his magazine? She was sorry, she replied; she feared she would 'always be a worry to the publishing world' – 'write to order I really cannot ... Indeed, if I may at all hope to be remembered, I would rather live as a single book writer than as an only-one-readable book writer'.

Periodically, she feared that the 'fire' had died out, and lamented that she knew no way of rekindling poetic coals. But she also knew that good poetry must be waited for, not willed.

Her brother Gabriel – a rather purplish poet as well as a poetic painter – described Christina as a more natural and 'spontaneous' writer than himself. Her other brother William claimed that her 'habits of composition' were 'entirely of the casual kind' – meaning that they flowed fully formed from her feelings. But this was because, as he admitted, he never saw her at work. From childhood, she kept her writing secret, until the composition was complete. 'Perhaps the nearest approach to a method I can lay claim to was a distinct aim at conciseness', she explained later; 'after a while I received a hint from my sister that my love of conciseness tended to make my writing obscure, and I then endeavoured to avoid obscurity as well as diffuseness'.

Her poems are seldom obscure, but they have what Angela Leighton has called a 'secret reserve of meaning, unidentified yet expressed', a note of riddling nonsense at the heart, which ironizes otherwise simple sentiments: 'I hang my harp upon a tree,/A weeping willow in a lake;/I hang my silenced harp there, wrung and snapt/For a dream's sake.//Lie still, lie still my breaking heart;/My silenced heart, lie still and break:/Life, and the world, and mine own self, are changed/For a dream's sake'.

Pre-eminent as a poet of grief, she was also wry and witty. Thus 'Promises like Piecrust' are made to be broken:

If I promised, I believe,
I should fret to break the chain.
Let us be the friends we were,
Nothing more but nothing less;
Many thrive on frugal fare
Who would perish of excess.

Pope as much as Keats was a key influence. So too were Beddoes and Poe, contributing to the Gothick strain in which Rossetti wrote of nightmares, of being buried alive, of goblins, crocodiles and ghostly revenants. In her later years she studied Dante (the family banshee, as William called him) and Petrarch, turning the sonnet convention round to give voice to a woman's desire for an unattainable man.

Surprisingly for such a well anthologized writer, there was no collected edition of her poems (and none at all of her sparkling short stories) between 1904 and the three-volume variorum version from Louisiana University Press, completed in 1990. C.H. Sisson's small but valuable Carcanet selection (1984) is complemented by a couple of 'giftbook' collections, but Rossetti deserves to be better known than as a minor Pre-Raphaelite in the shadow of her more-famous brother, or – *pace* Margaret Thatcher's invocation of 'Up-hill' – as the poet of dismal, self-denying Victorian values.

Her life was troubled, and her spirit 'sorely wrung' by depression and fear of damnation. But by this token she speaks to a troubled modern age. On Tennyson's death in 1892, Lewis Carroll (whose own Alice was partly inspired by 'Goblin Market') had no doubt who was the finest living poet. 'If only the Queen would consult me as to whom to make Poet Laureate!' he wrote, 'I would say "For once, Madam, take a *lady*!"'

Sadly, he was not asked, and there has as yet been no female Laureate. But in this centenary year of her death on 29 December 1894, a revaluation of Christina Rossetti's work is surely in order. Who else could write like this? 'I dreamt I caught a little owl/And the bird was blue ...'

**Jan Marsh's *Christina Rossetti: A Literary Biography* will be published by Cape in September; she is also preparing an edition of Rossetti's poetry and short fiction for Everyman paperbacks.**

*Illustration by Polly Joannu, Central St Martin's School of Art*

## SUJATA BHATT
### *The Stinking Rose*

Everything I want to say is
in that name
for these cloves of garlic – they shine
like pearls still warm from a woman's neck.

My fingernail nudges and nicks
the smell open, a round smell
    that spirals up.  Are you hungry?
Does it burn through your ears?

Did you know some cloves were planted
near the coral-coloured roses
to provoke the petals
into giving stronger perfume . . .

Everything is in that name
         for garlic:
Roses and smells
    and the art of naming . . .

*What's in a name? that which we call a rose,*
*By any other name would smell as sweet . . .*

But that which we call garlic
smells sweeter, more
vulnerable, even delicate
if we call it *The Stinking Rose.*

The roses on the table, the garlic in the salad
and the salt teases our ritual
tasting to last longer.
You who dined with us tonight,
this garlic will sing to your heart
to your slippery muscles – will keep
your nipples and your legs from sleeping.

Fragrant blood full of garlic –
yes, they noted it reeked under the microscope.

His fingers tired after peeling and crushing
the stinking rose, the sticky cloves –
Still, in the middle of the night his fingernail
nudges and nicks her very own smell,
    her prism open –

*This is the title poem of Sujata Bhatt's next collection, to be published by
Carcanet in early 1995.*

## LINDA FRANCE
### *Meteorology*

Afterwards she blamed it on the wind, cold
in the air like someone's breath in her ear.
And listening was the mistake she made,
wishing its wild stories were really true.
The almanac they consulted lied,
its wicked lips closing and opening,
an oracle of storms, mercury trapped
in blue glass. And afterwards that something
had happened, something beginning with **m**,
was all she knew, that tasted like the wind,
smoke and citrus, someone else's perfume.
The weather changed: something lost, something gained,
the rain, filled the space between them, so far
apart, buckets and buckets of weather.

*Linda France's first collection,* **Red,** *was published by Bloodaxe in 1992; she is the
editor of* **Sixty Women Poets** *(Bloodaxe, 1993).*

# Dead Society Poet

### Brendan O'Keeffe views the T.S. Eliot biopic, Tom and Viv

It has been put about that *Tom and Viv* – about T. S. Eliot's first marriage – is largely the story of a singular individual who midwifed far-reaching and prescriptive modernist poetry; who inspired without being inspired; who had much to say but little technique to write; whose mental state was unstable and who was the power behind the lionized poet. In fact, Ezra Pound isn't even mentioned.

The film – coauthored by Michael Hastings who adapts his own stage play – shows the tortured Vivienne Haigh-Wood rewriting the poet's work and providing him with the title for *The Waste Land*. Even if you're not aware that its veracity has subsequently been demolished, you don't trust director Brian Gilbert from the first scene, an ominous use of one of the hoariest conventions of the British period drama. A vintage motor chugs down a country lane. As it draws near some cycling soldiers, who sport the first of the beige trousers that distressingly dominate the movie, one's heart is in one's mouth. Will the extras pretend that a vehicle hurtling along at 25 mph is unsettling their Sunday dawdle? As the car passes, reassuringly they affect consternation. Ah, the headlong speed of the machine age.

This kind of brittle naivety is mistaken for period charm throughout. Equally listless are the dim interiors, monotonous pace, laughable symbolism. There are no voiceover banalities, but plenty of square lines of dialogue. The no-nonsense script sometimes throws out a few teasers for literary smart-alecks: 'That's not what I meant at all', Tom rebukes Viv, whose nerves are bad again tonight. Yes, bad.

Willem Dafoe, as 'Tom' Eliot, is a versatile actor who came to prominence as the sensitive hippie pothead sergeant in *Platoon*. Here he fights off the squadrons of undisciplined emotion with taut facial control and serial killer specs. His repression works well against the overstimulated Miranda Richardson as Viv. As Eliot takes his exalted place in literary society, he is shown discarding the difficult Viv – whose hormonal illness causes mania – like a botched stanza. Richardson, who has the ability to create a character in her first appearance, goes on to give an overblown, actressy performance. She is directed to trash rooms, pull a knife on Virginia Woolf, retort bitterly, wring her hands a lot, and she duly obliges. Her tense pallor and sheer bloody screechiness leave you feeling cramped, and Brian Gilbert's static, pictorially-composed direction increases the yearning for fresh air and honest emotions.

Anyone who finds this faction plausible (and it is) should try and get hold of an interview Eliot's second wife, Valerie, gave to Blake Morrison

(*Independent on Sunday*, 24.4.94). Not a disinterested witness, it's true, but one who, with dignified reluctance, furnishes various documentary proofs that both play and film have no credibility as fact. Key episodes from the first marriage are misrepresented or invented: the list, like life, is very long. Obviously the opportunity to see Valerie Eliot's refutation isn't available to most viewers, and so the film, aimed at a general audience for all its occasional literary allusions, is an act of contumely against the late Eliot.

There is an attempt to show that much of his work was based on reminiscences, but no indication that such 'personal grumbles' were planted, hauntingly, as unexplicated depth-charges. Gilbert and Hastings have no sense of the stresses of poetic thinking other than cheap surface emblems. So a poet is someone slumped over a typewriter who gets a boring job and sometimes plays musical chairs with Bloomsbury nobs. Eliot's dictum of impersonality is quoted but not thrown into ironic relief or even examined. Most of all, there's no acknowledgement that a poet, certainly this poet, is not dedicated to the surface of his or her life and cares intensely about what does not, in material terms, matter.

Are both film and play sops to a distorted kind of post-Plath feminism or is there some obscure grudge Hastings in particular harbours against Eliot, his politics, former critical dictatorship, his poetic reputation? *Tom and Viv*'s iconoclasm about the man is exceeded by its iconolatry towards the woman.

## DERYN REES-JONES
### *And Please Do Not Presume*

And please do not presume it was the way we planned it,
Nor later say *We might have tried harder,*
Or *Could have done better.*
Nor remind us of the things we didn't take:
The hints, the trains, the tonics,
The tape-recordings of ourselves asleep,
The letters of a previous lover,
The photos of each other as a child.

And please do not presume our various ways of making up,
Of telling lies and truths, the way we touched
Or laughed, the Great Mistakes, the Tiger Suit,
Our list of *Twenty Favourite Movie Classics,*
Breakfast in bed, red wine, the different ways we tried
To make each other come
Were anything else than the love we wanted;

Or that we did no more or less than anybody might have done.

And more, do not presume we could have stopped it —
Like a clock, a gap, a leak, or rot; or made it
Last much longer than it did;
Or that the note on the fridge that one of us left
Wasn't sweetly meant, but badly spelt:
*Step One of Ten Proggressive Ways to Disolution.*

**Deryn Rees-Jones won a Gregory Award last year. Her first collection, The Memory Tray, will be published by Seren this autumn.**

# French Roulette

*Stephen Romer on the word-gambler supreme, Stéphane Mallarmé.*

**Gordon Millan,**
*Mallarmé: A Throw of the Dice,*
Secker & Warburg, £30,
ISBN 0 436 27096 X

Two weeks after Stéphane Mallarmé's funeral, his daughter Genevieve came across a pencilled note wedged into his pad of blotting paper which gave instructions that all his unpublished papers should be burned. This last letter, written out of a presentiment of his sudden death at the age of 56, bears poignant testimony to the wreck of that hypothetical Great Work with which he had tantalized his contemporaries for so many years. 'There is no literary heritage, my children. Do not even submit anything to the gaze of any other person. Refuse any action proposed out of curiosity or friendship. Say that there is nothing to be discovered in these papers, moreover that is the truth, and you, my poor prostrate creatures, the only people in the world capable of respecting to such an extent the whole life's work of a sincere artist, believe me when I say that it was all going to be so beautiful'. Set beside this Paul Gaugin's statement, on hearing of the poet's death – 'the most beautiful part of his work was his life' – and you reach the heart of a familiar paradox. At Mallarmé's funeral, Henri Roujon, speaking on behalf of the older generation, said much the same, to tear-jerking effect – 'He would offer you a friendly hand and at the same time lower his eyelids over those enormous child-like eyes'. Gordon Millan, in this new biography of Mallarmé, claims to see a 'fundamental unity' between his life and his work. It is as if they shine out like twin stars in a unique constellation that is Stéphane Mallarmé – *Tel qu'en Lui-même enfin l'éternité le change;* and yet one could argue that his Great Work bears more resemblance to the *Chef-d'oeuve inconnu* – an incomprehensible tangle of signs, with one or two perfectly achieved details.

Mallarmé lived with the possibility of failure every day of his life – why else his appeal, in that last note, to his good faith and sincerity as an artist? Another letter to a friend, written at the end of his life, makes a confession tragic in its implication. Having shut himself away in Valvins, his country retreat near Fontainebleau, Mallarmé describes how he devotes his mornings adding 'jottings for the dream', intended for the Great Work, and his afternoons trying to complete 'Herodiade', the poem

that for some thirty years nearly 'sterilized' him. 'It is all rather a waste of time living behind closed shutters', he admits in this letter. 'A lethargy settles within me which can be felt materially in the pen itself'. True, he had only recently completed *Un Coup de des* and his prose volume *Divagations,* but even so it is a discomforting admission from a man who had spent so much of his life craving time and solitude, and actively loathing any duties – most of all teaching – that deprived him of them. Mallarmé certainly never made a success of his 'professional' career ... Very early on, in a poem like 'Les Fenêtres', written in London in 1863, the poet drove a wedge between the Ideal and the Real – 'Mais, helas! Ici-bas est maitre' – and at the same time wrote to his friend Henri Cazalis, exhorting him to 'drink deep of the Ideal' and repel any happiness on offer 'ici-bas'. Gautier's bullish jibes at 'utilité', Laforgue's elegant complaint at 'la quotidienne' pale beside Mallarmé's passionately held conviction, kept alive throughout his life by his drudgery as English teacher at the Lycée. Rimbaud's great refusal is a different matter, and Mallarmé's measured description of him as that 'passant considerable' who wrote out of 'une puberté perverse et superbe' barely conceals his censure: art was a life sentence, and there was no evading it. By contrast, his acute distress at the news of Baudelaire's illness reveals the identity of his true exemplar.

Art for art's sake, the ideology of the time, goes some way to explaining Mallarmé's thirst for an ideal poetry of essences, or rather they give it a framework. But it cannot explain the uniqueness that Mallarmé, early on, claimed for himself, as very nearly the *only* poet of his time; the rest of them, like his original mentor des Essarts, he came to criticize for 'mixing' the Ideal with the Real. To turn to Millan's book for illumination on this is, unfortunately, to risk disappointment. Using material about the poet's childhood, unearthed since the last biography was written (some fifty years ago) might have given some clues, but Millan's account lacks conviction, and the cumulative effect of his caution not only leads to frustration but vitiates his style. Too often, we encounter plodding sentences like these, in which he attempts to gauge the effect on the boy of the death, first of his mother, and then of his beloved sister, Maria: 'A measure of caution is required here. We need to distrust the temptation (which too many critics have found irresistible) of exaggerating the personal impact of his mother's death upon the young Mallarmé [...] First, Mallarmé was only five years old when his mother died; the whole event may have seemed somewhat remote to him. Second [...] in the western Europe of the middle to late nineteenth century death at an early age was very much more commonplace than it is today'. Try telling that to a five year old who has just lost his mother! Responding to a letter from Cazalis, in which he enclosed a photograph of his English sweetheart Ettie Yapp, Mallarmé exclaims in a typically generous outburst: 'I'll put her in my heart next to the poor young ghost who for thirteen years was my sister and the only person I ever adored, before I met you all'. Millan explains this away as the product of 'a highly emotional point in Mallarmé's life (when he once again discovered what it was to have true friends of his own age)'. But his own supposedly psychological insight (Mallarmé's new friends) is itself open to question, and while his attempt to avoid an excessively psychoanalytic interpretation of his subject is creditable, he finds little to replace it with. Frequently, in his account of Mallarmé's early years, one is tempted to exclaim with Pound 'damn perhapses' – and 'seems' and 'maybes'! Astonishingly, the one opportunity he had to penetrate the way in which Mallarmé coped with personal grief, written out as it is in some compelling, heart-rending notes, is missed. The notes in question, made after the death of his son and collected posthumously under the title *Pour un Tombeau d'Anatole* constitute a key-text, crucial to our understanding of Mallarmé. In Millan's book, this text, to which I shall return, is consigned to a footnote.

To be fair, things improve when we reach the more solidly documented period of Mallarmé's marriage, and his years of provincial exile as a teacher in Tournon, Besançon and Avignon. His marriage to Maria Gerhard, a German governess, seven years his senior, and of a lower class, with whom he eloped to London in 1863, surprised his friends who had all advised him against such a move – often for snobbish reasons. If we are to believe Mallarmé's letters, he married her not from the daring of a moment's surrender, but from a sense of duty: 'If I were marrying Marie to ensure my own happiness, I would be quite mad. Besides, is happiness obtainable on this earth? ... No, I am marrying Marie solely because I know that without me she will not be able to live and because I have poisoned her pure existence', he explained in a letter. Although Maria of the doleful countenance – so pleasing to Mallarmé – seems to disappear from Millan's story, it does seem to have been a solid, loving marriage. Later on, it is true, Mallarmé was to cultivate the friendship, and briefly become the lover, of the sometime actress Mary Laurent, whom he cast deliberately and half-playfully as the Muse of many sonnets and *eventails*.

Mallarmé resisted the earnest hopes of his relations, solid civil servants in the Ministry of Finance, that he would continue the tradition. He opted instead for the Ministry of Education, but the series of scathing reports from a whole string of headmasters and school inspectors about his performance as a teacher prompts one to ask if he wouldn't have been better off in an office. In 1866, the same year as the famous *Crise de Tournon*, in which Mallarmé made metaphysical and linguistic discoveries of frightening implication, and laid the foundations of his Great Work, a school inspector complained that in the poet's 'first year Special Education course, fourteen pupils all working together could not translate for me "Give me some bread and water"'. There was never enough money either, though his attempts to earn more by 'outrageous publications' were frowned upon. And when he got home at the end of the day – to Eliot home from the bank or Larkin from the library, add Mallarmé from the Lycee – 'I burst into tears when I feel a total void within myself and when I am unable to place a single word on my impeccably white sheet of paper'.

In the end, he did write, and the effects of what he wrote, during those lonely nights of vigil in Tournon, in his little study overlooking the Rhône, are with us still. Millan describes the Crise de Tournon straightforwardly and with restraint, which is admirable in itself, given the welter of excited speculation Mallarmé's spectacular 'linguistic turn' has provoked in writers like Blanchot and Sartre and Derrida. (There is of course more to it than he suggests, and I am sorry that he chooses not to mention Yves Bonnefoy's magisterial *Preface* to the authoritative recent Gallimard/Poche edition of the *Poésies*). As well as sketching out *Herodiade*, Mallarmé was also making those extraordinary statements in letters to Cazalis, unique in all literature: 'I have to let you know that I am now impersonal and no longer the Stéphane whom you used to know. I am instead an aptitude of the Spiritual Universe which permits the latter to become visible and develop itself through the person who I used to be'. One is curious to know how Stéphane's old confidant, Henri Cazalis, replied to this born-again 'aptitude'.

The rest of Mallarmé's life consisted in trying to stay true to his essential vision, and also in trying to live up to the impossible rigours his Great Work required of him. It is no accident that most of what he did publish were occasional, often commissioned pieces. Never, probably, has a writer gained so much prestige from a non-existent work; but on countless Tuesday evenings, his *Mardis* in Paris, when he received some of the most distinguished artists of his time, and welcomed a new generation into the circle – Valéry, Gide, Louys – he kept his dream alive in their heads by the brilliance of his conversation. Millan marches us through the years of Mallarmé's fame, with their friendships and banquets, but the inner man goes missing along the

way. More attention was needed to a text like this, from *Pour un Tombeau d'Anatole*: 'lutte/des deux/père et fils/l'un pour/Conserver fils en/pensée – ideal -/l'autre pour/vivre, se relevant...' That is a terrible acknowledgement – of the struggle between the idealizing poet-father who wants to conserve his son in thought – and the dead son himself, who wants to live again, flesh and blood.

**Stephen Romer's latest collection is *Plato's Ladder* (Oxford Poets)**

### MIMI KHALVATI
### *Au Jardin du Luxembourg (detail)*

#### *after Henri Cross*

If summer had its ghosts, gifts of wind
wind blows to you and whisks away,
then these two small girls

in pale pink flared
like two sweetpeas
I would take for mine and twirl them
to the balustrade . . .

Look, how squatting, peering down
they think the ground a river,
a winding in the gravel

whose underwater mysteries
like gaps between our memories
appear and disappear . . .

Like gaps between our memories
that reappear through tow-ropes
seemingly in reach, then, far out

where leaves are light
and light is fish
persuade us with a colour,
dissuade us with a depth

twirl them back through leaflitter,
parkland, crossroads, up and over
chimney stacks, birchsmoke, lavender

till, like gaps between our memories,
seed and dust and all wind carries,
they are seen at such a distance

we think them elemental
light, fire, air!

## PENELOPE SHUTTLE

# *Waterlily Tradition*

The women are singing in the patisserie,
their faces pencilled
by doubts, diets and genre friendships,

but he composes better songs
skinnydipping beautifully in my lily pond,
lolling against the Lucida and the Perry's Pink.

I wonder what else he will do to make me
feel so strange – there are so many possibilities.

While he floats and composes like a foundling
among copulant dragonflies and sleepy slithering terrapins,
I worry that nothing will last, nothing!

But then, remembering other lives I never speak about,
I feel more cheerful, and drift out
to my trustful garden where at the waterside
young Rossini is slicking back

his damp dago curls.  How honestly he consumes
my candied patronage! He takes my hand,
glad to be haunted by me, and tells me,

'Childhood is often close to the waterlily
tradition – ruthless floating innocence,
Madame, too beautiful, too observed . . .'

What he says must be true, I know this,
just as I know one day he will betray me.
But for today I am content to be in tune with young Rossini

who says he can smell water a mile off
like a horse, and who composes best with rain on his lips.
He kisses me . . .

Now do you believe me when I say I love to sing?
It is my waterlily tradition.

*Penelope Shuttle's latest collection,* **Taxing the Rain,** *is reviewed on page 81.*

# Serious Play Syndrome

*Miroslav Holub has triumphantly escaped the tag, 'East European poet'. His use of science and his classic Czech drollery give him a unique perspective on the New Europe.* **David Morley** *and* **Kevan Johnson** *spoke to him during a recent visit to London:*

**DM**: I'd like to begin by asking you two questions from your poem 'Conversation with a Poet' – *Are you a poet?* and *How do you know?*

**MH**: I would say I was never sure first of all. There are different kinds of poets. There are people who 'feel themselves to be poets' and, as you may know from the recent publications, there is a high percentage of 'real poets' who are prone to develop some sort of neurosis, or some sort of cyclic psychosis ... The neurosis rate of 'real poets' – and I admire them, I am not mocking them – may indicate that there is a kind of psychological disposition attached to poetry. I am definitely not this kind of poet! For scientific workers, the probability of the cyclic psychosis is below average compared to a normal population. So, I think I am too normal to be a 'real poet'. I would never label myself as a poet.

**DM**: You've been described by Alvarez as 'one of the sanest voices of our time' and, to some poets you seem to be saying, this might be a disqualification ...

**MH**: Yes! Yes.

**DM**: How does that wear? A sane voice?

**MH**: Well, there is a deeper sort of personal question involved. Are you – is your life supposed to be sacrificed for literature? I have the feeling that I would rather live my life than to sacrifice it. If there is one word I hate in the English language it is 'workaholic' . I 'work' almost all the time, but I would hate more than being labelled as a poet to be labelled a workaholic because I think it's a sort of deviation: basically, as we're born human our obligation is to stay human, not to turn into some kind of black, manic engine. So, I still never say I spend sixteen hours a day 'working'. Well, eight hours a day working, the rest I spend just looking around – being, and especially what I like most in life, and that's playing.

**DM**: Do you regard the poetry as work or play or both?

**MH**: Some poets have already made the statement that poetry is basically a game. It's play. Of course, very serious play. I would say that humans are the only zoological species who play in adult life. For us, especially in poetry, we try to redeem our child-hoods ... there is something very childish about poetry, starting with the full concentration of the play and the joy, the sensation of the joy of the poem. We are the only zoological species which uses play as a life realization activity. For any cat, for any tiger, for any elephant, play is a preparation for an adult life which is struggle, a fight for survival, for food, and so on. But we use the game because we've got rid of these 'animal-connections', these animal-relations to our environment. So, we are the only playing animal.

**KJ:** At the reading last night you were asked how your writing had changed since 1989, and what you were writing about now. You said your subject was the same – it was idiocy. Previously there was only one type of idiocy – the communist regime – but now idiocy comes in 57 varieties.

**MH:** On all sides of political and human life in a totalitarian regime you have dull people and smart people. But in a totalitarian system you have a tremendous advantage: that in the reigning establishment stupidity is so dominant that you can forget the other stupidities. They don't count so much. And, basically, you can feel an ally of some simple-minded people who may not be too bright but they have the same issue at heart: to corrode the dominant stupidity. You can corrode one stupidity with another stupidity. In a free, open society, the democratic society, you are concerned with all the possible deviations from the same thing. One of the consequences of the former system was that the people now started to go in for all sorts of alternative thinking. For example, science, experimental science or basic research, existed in the communist regime. Because it existed, people thought something must be wrong even with the basic research; there must be some alternative way to acquire knowledge. This is, for me, a nonsense, but a nonsense follows from the former conditions. It's because you didn't have a choice, and now you have a choice – an immense number of choices! If we are to find some way to survive in the modern world, the technological world, we must be very disciplined ... For me, freedom means observing the rules, provided the rules are being put rationally and they've got common consent. Not to observe the rules is anarchy.

**DM**: I'd like to ask you about kindness. You've said in an essay ('On Kindness', *The Dimension of the Present Moment*): 'Only through kindness can exams in biochemistry, like life itself, become memorable', and through the kindness of your examiner you achieved a B-minus. In an age of ethnic cleansing on the one hand and talk of a new world order on the other, what mark would you give the human race?

**MH**: I wouldn't give them an A-plus, more a B-plus. With an A-plus it would be the end of evolution, it can't be done ... I take kindness as a very broad quality which may not serve any purpose. There is something about being human which means you don't behave in human relations with a biological purposefulness. Culturally, we should be subjected to another kind of Darwinian selection – not the aggressive force for survival, but the force for kindness. In some situations we are selected for it – I like all human meetings which select or put a pressure on myself to be simply human in this sense. Not to win, and not to display your colours, but just to display your ability to be in proximity with other people.

**DM**: This is an aspect of what Richard Dawkins called 'memes', units of culture being passed from brian to brain within cultural evolution, isn't it – selection through a social or cultural situation?

**MH**: Yes, and those pressures are significant. I would say that in my poetry I miss the pressure of kindness sometimes. I would like to put an internal onus on myself to write in terms of kindness. I don't think I've learnt to be warm or kind enough. I must always supress a pedagogic or sterile approach to things, topics and people.

**DM**: What research are you working on at the moment? How are the infamous nude mice?

**MH**: I'm working with great difficulty. Thank you for asking, but the nude mice are not well; there are not enough funds for the nude mice. My task for the next few months is to find new accomodation for my mice colonies. Unfortunately, the subject I'm working on now is one of the very few innovative scientific ideas I've ever had – that is the influence of cool ambient temperature on immune functions. Before coming here I applied for a grant to support a new working group just to finish some of the work off. You never do 'finish', of course; you will never finish by saying 'The cold is simply *this*'. It could just be another complication in the solution of the problem that is 'catching cold'. Basically, if you catch cold it means that your immune defenses have been somewhere, somehow, weakened. The poor, formerly socialist, Nude Mouse – now today's Democratic Nude Mouse – is a beautiful tool because it simply, easily caught cold; it's like experimenting on a naked human, a 'naked ape'.

**DM**: Can we talk about your education? Were you ever taught to feel any sharp disparity between scientific training and the arts?

**MH**: It's a very important knot. I was educated in a Classical Gymnasium, a high school for Greek and Latin. Within the lessons of Greek language and grammar, our professor taught us Greek philosophy, Greek geometry, and the basics of Greek science, which was marvellous. In these lessons it was all one culture. He was a memorable personality and in any education system so much depends upon the personalities. I feel the only thing one can do about the education system is to have good teachers. I had good teachers, and at university some memorable personalities who would not show you how stupid you are as a student but would be kind to you, and push you ahead, and that's exactly what a personality does.

We had a mathematician who was also teaching theoretical physics and, at the same time, was a musician. Professor Spelda was his name. Very much the one culture man, he was an active musician, he was reviewing cultural events in my native town of Pilsen, and he was a very educated mathematician and physicist. But I had some oustanding teachers at University who actually never 'taught' us. I had a physiologist, Professor Laufberger, who never actually taught human or general physiology. Most of the time he developed his personal theory on nervous impulses. He was dominated by the theory, it was his obsession, and he was so obsessed with this theory that he made it something memorable. Even the less gifted student must be impressed with such a personality.

I had a great professor of surgery, Jirdsek. He always would bring – it was a most a dramatic effect – he would bring a patient on a stretcher or an amputated leg or a tumour in a dish and make a lecture on this topic. In one lecture it would be the surgery of the knee and another time it was abdominal surgery, another it was brain surgery ... it didn't have any coherence but we will never forget it. And he was speaking with us, which was a kindness. He would speak with us as with colleagues and not as dull students. So I was very lucky with my education. It was 1948 when the communists took over. Then most of these professors lost their jobs and were replaced by some typical, mediocre teachers trying to teach, but conveying no passion.

**DM:** What astonishes me about your life is the ease in which you feel within what we still call The Two Cultures – what Medawar calls 'this idiotic debate'. A teacher's force of personality aside, are there any concrete criteria you would suggest for reconciling the cultures?

**MH:** It's partly a problem of expense, it's the cost. In the United States you have a very interesting, very intensive university career by which you are deeply embodied in the community, in your type of school, in your type of college and hardly have time to move to another place. We were much more free. As I've said, even as a medical student I had time enough to listen to Professor Patocka, the philosopher, albeit he was a phenomenologist. I still don't understand him though. I mastered the intellectual method but I am not sure I know what it is about. It's exactly like Einstein – my colleague, Einstein [laughs] – he said the same thing: 'Whenever I hear philosophy I feel I have to swallow something which I haven't had on my tongue'. But we have been free to move from one culture to another and back. And under the conditions of a totalitarian system you feel more or less on one ship – all the system is based on the class struggle. All the people with higher education would feel on the ship compared with the reigning idiocy; just trying to get away or just trying to corrode the reigning monolithic idiocy. And, therefore, all kinds of cultural activity, be it scientific, be it literary or artistic regard themselves as biologically necessary and interconnected. Not in every society are you persuaded into feeling connected like this. So one remedy for the two cultures difficulty would be just to get yourself a good totalitarian system! [laughs]

**DM:** One of the statements you made in 1963 seems very related to William Carlos Williams's ethic of ideas. You say your outlook was achieved by what you called 'no longer the traditionally lyrical or the magically illogical but the energy, tension and illumination contained within the fact itself'. Do you still stick with that or have you changed?

**MH:** No. I wouldn't change the quotation. I would still subscribe to it – albeit since the 1970s the development of the bulk of Czech poetry has been towards the poetry of the Ego or Id, or the poetry of silence. There is no clear (I hate the word) *message*, philosophical or political message. I love real, playful nonsense in modern poetry.

> **'One remedy for the two cultures difficulty would be just to get yourself a good totalitarian system!'**

But, still, it must be something transparent. There should be a poetic idea in *my* system, in *my* thinking which is far from being a common sense ethic, far from a philosophical idea, far from the scientific idea. But, still, it is a backbone to the poem and with all the images, with all the variation, with all the play of imagination, you are still arriving somewhere! Maybe the description of the ethos is 'the poetry *aiming* somewhere'. I wouldn't define where, but aiming somewhere. The worst hermetic poetry is aimless, just thickets of words, words which may be beautiful but have at least one bad connotation: they can't be translated, they can't be transferred.

**KJ:** You were speaking earlier of passionate, broad-minded teachers. In this country there are a growing number of creative writing courses teaching poetry; in the States there are many more. You've written of poets in '50s Czechoslovakia: 'We entered literature by shutting up, by complete silence, by complete distrust of everyone. It was a perfect lesson in creative non-writing'. Do you think poetry can be taught? Can creative writing be approached in a useful way?

**MH:** One thing is suspicious: is poetry the last thing in the twentieth or twenty-first century which shouldn't be taught, which doesn't really need any technical education? Every violinist, every composer, every painter, must pass through some university schooling ... Why not writers? So this is one disbalance with writing. Therefore some kind of technical education may be needed. In our condition this technical education is usually conveyed by the colleagues. Also, most of the future writers come from the school of philosophy, through their Bohemistic departments and they are in professional groups and try to write criticism and make up some sort of creative writing together with theory. The second education is by the editors and senior writers in the publishing houses and magazines. So this is some sort of creative writing pressure already. Why not teach what that's about?

But the second question: can poetry be taught? Of course not. But can painting be taught? Of course not? Can music be taught? Can you educate a Beethoven? *It* must be there but you need some technical education and you need to be introduced into 'the inner realm', and with some, the good creative writing programmes, they do it. As I've already written in one essay, the greatest input of creative writing is as a rule a negative one. You persuade the really hopeless students to stop, otherwise too many survive and infest the scene with writing that either overburdens people or has no readers, and which requires forces and energies which that writer could have used usefully in some other profession; these are people who should be persuaded to stop. I think the best creative writing would include as many individual consultations as were possible. I've taught creative writing in the States and in Prague – in the Central European University. It's much easier for me to do it in Prague because I have the backing of the city of Kafka! But in any creative writing there is a very direct connection between the writer and the student, and the teaching itself is very beneficial for the teacher, for their imagination through their understanding of the students, of the system of thinking of the students. So in the same way for the student towards the teacher. I have a very positive attitude towards creative writing.

**DM:** Between 1970 and 1980, you became effectively a non-person because of your signing a petition. How do you know you've become a non-person and when do you know you've become a person again? What are the physical mechanisms and the political strategies involved?

**MH:** It's through a very concrete situation. I became a non-person on the day I was called to the publishing house where my book on Edgar Allan Poe was supposed to appear and I was told: 'From now on you can't be named. Your name, like so many others, must disappear, but the book must appear because, after all, it cost us 600,000 crowns! So you must accept that the book will appear without your name'. And from that moment I thought that I knew I was a non-person. As a non-person I was supposed to offer an apology or recantation, but I never did. The whole thing was a police provocation, an *agent provocateur* situation. But as a non-person anyway I had very little defence. So I was a double non-person: not only not writing but also writing some things which I hadn't written. It was a double negation of existence. Later on, in the '80s, even the Party bosses got a little more relaxed. I wouldn't say it was a liberation in the '80s but you could sense some change. One day in 1980 I was called by a friendly editor, he said: 'Look, we may now find a way to publish these non-persons: we can publish one element per year. So we will start off with another Czech poet or yourself. Which do you think?' So I said 'Start off with the other because he's older and secondly he needs the money' (because I still was in the laboratory and the other poet was nowhere). So he

began with one poet and next year it was me, just one element a year but that is the Czech way. Finally, the bosses ... they get tired when you insist, when you use the great Czech strategy: 'The water could excavate the stone, not by force, but by frequent falling'. So the bosses would give up because you would ask them the same question, pose the same problem time and time again; they would say No! once but not 15 times. So finally the situation was – with the exception of the full dissidents like Havel – even the 'less dangerous' would have been allowed to publish without the 1989 breakthrough. I have actually seen in 1988 the programme of one publishing house where there was already a Kundera. It was another attempt. Again the censors would say 'No, think of the cost! – Kundera, no'. The next day they would say 'Kundera? OK'. That was the policy.

**DM:** You're now living in the Czech Republic. I'd like to quote from your poem 'Wenceslas Square Syndrome' which was written before the Velvet Revolution: 'But from the linden that forgot/ to lose its leaves resounds a blackbird's mighty voice,/ the song rises and drops into the subway,/ song of the only December schizophrenic blackbird,/ mighty, everlasting song of the only/schizophrenic blackbird,/ yes, of course,/ a song'. How has the velvet revolution affected matters for younger poets? Have you found yet a mood of optimism among them?

**MH:** There have been young poets – with the exception of the full dissidents – who had greater possibilities for being printed before the revolution than they have now. Before the revolution they would be introduced into the reading circuit; there was a heavy, intensive programme of reading for the young ones. At one point they had the beautiful name of 'the green feathers'. *Green feathers*. Nowadays it's very different, it's very hard to publish any poem. So many of the young, not only poets, but artists, are growing a little sour about it. I was on a programme on Australian ABC television about Prague. They interviewed a couple of young artists, and also me, and I was the only optimistic guy on the programme! I said that the real artists would survive under the new economic pressures with all its dangers of the consumer society, and the commercial culture coming in. But most of the young artists would say 'We are very disappointed: we thought that with the playwright Havel as a president ... We hoped he would see that we would be financially supported but we aren't'. But that's the price of freedom as I understand it. We all had the foolish expectation that the 'good, Western capitalist' would immediately support our economy. Whereas, of course, they are suppressing it because it is competition and we are a weaker economy. We can't produce as much steel as we could, we can't export as much meat as we did because of EC regulations. That's the price we pay so that the poet can say what he wants to say, not what he was supposed to say. To complain is one thing, but young artists should do something about it. That means for instance trying to be more comprehensible ... I would say the potential reader of poetry per capita is still not such a rare animal in our conditions, but we have to approach him, we have to attract him. We can't go on just being as post-communist, post-modernist and post-dissident as possible. I always say that post-communist post-modernists tend to be much harsher than the simple post-modernist. The former is a post-modernist with a personal touch, and with a personal mission. Modernism was communist. Now we are post-communist, anti-communist post-modernists! With all kinds of ideological and structural minimalistical features which are beyond plain people.

**KJ:** That's very different from, say, the American model where post-modernism can mean a more relaxed attitude towards modernism. I always think that a post-modernist is a modernist who no longer *worries* about the modern. Post-communist post-modernism sounds ridden with political angst.

**MH:** I would say that out post-modernism is too influenced by the French Derridean attitude towards truth, towards knowledge, towards progress. The sentence is what counts, the speech is what counts, not the message. I just wish there was just more fun in the post-modern condition. But I see it turning into something priest-like again. I think they are taking themselves extremely seriously.

**KJ:** You've said you'd like people to read your poems, or to read poetry, as naturally as they would go to a football match.

**MH:** Well, well. This was a juvenile dream. It can't be done but still it could be the direction. The direction you take in poetry needs to be as comprehensible as possible, and to use aesthetic qualities which can be shared with other people. One of the main aesthetic qualities in present day writing is humour. We have a great education in the political joke. We survive by joking. I even suspect that something we have in common in England and the Czech Republic is the way of joking. We understand the English way of joking. It is strange how it's developed because we never had any ties with England until the war. We started to shift culturally, aesthetically, emotionally to the English speaking world, from Paris. It can't be chance that so many of the best Czech translators translated American and English poetry. Since the war, in the last forty years, with all the communists around, we had four big anthologies of American poetry, three big anthologies of British poetry, in addition to poets in single volumes, plus a special magazine which published translated poetry only. So we had everybody, even the younger poets, already translated. The most translated literature in Czech is the Anglo-American literature and there must be some reason for this.

**KJ:** Are there any modern British poets that you enjoy?

**MH:** Ted Hughes, Tony Harrison, Anthony Thwaite. I like Galway Kinnell, Ferlinghetti from the Americans. Usually when I read a book in English or American I feel I could translate him: with the aid of a dictionary, I understand him. When I read anyone from France or Italy, I don't feel I could translate him because I really don't know what he means. For example, the French style today is almost academic; it's very abstract compared with most of your poetry or our poetry from the '60s. There is a trend at the moment to try to go closer to the French poetic system. I was amazed at how different the literatures are, how different the poetic contexts are, by seeing my French book which may now be in print: the poems selected are ones which I wouldn't have translated into English. The conditions for French and English translation seem to be pretty much opposite.

**KJ:** What do you think English and Czech writers share?

**MH:** Irony, concrete thinking, some type of scepticism, some kind of cold-faced but warm-hearted cynicism. These qualities are quite unlike the subtle lyricism of the French.

**DM:** Lastly, could you tell us something about your next book, *Pilsen*?

**MH:** It's a mixture of poems and prose-poems concerned with the city of Pilsen. It's not geography, not history, it's very personal – it's my childhood. But the publishers must decide if it works in English. It wouldn't work without the photographs which I've included because our cities now are a mixture of delapidation and hope, new problems, new structures. The changing face of the city is part of us, part of our hopes and memories.

---

*Pilsen, Czechoslovakia and Myself* will be published by Bloodaxe Books later this year.

# Good Companion?

Ian Hamilton's Oxford Companion to Twentieth Century Poetry (OUP, £25, ISBN 0 19 866 147 9) had an easy passage through the national press. We asked five poets and critics to look a little deeper.

## BILL TURNER

We turn to reference books when we wish to check facts, or to augment our knowledge with more detail. How useful to have a volume where we can find out who first published any poet, and the title of his/her first collection. With a title eluding the tip of one's tongue, how practical to be able to tug out this companion from its niche between Chambers and Shakespeare to refresh one's memory!

So I turn to BARTLETT, Elizabeth, while wondering whether Hamilton has listed the American of the same name as well as our formidable and much loved author of *A Lifetime of Dying, Strange Territory, The Czar is Dead,* and *Instead of a Mass.* But hold on – there's nothing between BARKER and BAUGHAN! She's not included; it's an outrage! But perhaps I have chanced on an isolated lapse that will be rectified in the paperback edition? Now, what was the title of the Geoffrey Holloway collection published after *Rhine Jump?* Here's HOLLO, Anselm and then HOLLOWAY, John. No sign of a Geoffrey. This is incredible! But rapidly I discover that Sydney Tremayne's seven collections are ignored, while such popular poets as Elma Mitchell, Anna Adams, Connie Bensley, and John Latham are also excluded.

Even more frustrating than the inexcusable omissions are the extremely patchy notes on matters such as the Pulitzer prizes. Surely it should not have been beyond the person allocated this task to list in order all of the winning poets? What we get instead is the information that 'winners include ...' and we are offered a score of names pointedly excluding the two black poets, Gwendolyn Brooks and Rita Dove.

The grudging paragraph on *Poetry Review* contains the only mention of the Poetry Society, and no indication of the editorial initiative of Muriel Spark and John Smith, another unfairly ignored poet. No mention is made of the temporary editors who found the post a convenient stepping-stone to more prestigious employment.

Prolonged scrutiny of those chosen to supply notes on poets deemed worthy of inclusion reveals a blatant bias favouring Oxford-indoctrinated males apparently dedicated to the idea of rewriting literary history in their own favour. This preponderance of earnest academics touts such self-regarding promotions as the Movement's *New Lines* anthology of 1956 as important, while the countering anthology *Mavericks,* edited by Abse and Sergeant is ignored, although nearly 400 people subscribed to it in advance of publication.

So what is the minimal qualification for inclusion in this volume? In the entry for B.S. Johnson, we learn that his entire poetic output added up to sixty-three pieces. If Mick Imlah's arithmetic is sound this invites speculation that perhaps Johnson is only included so that someone with even less poetic output than Imlah or Hamilton can be highlighted.

On the factual level, the entry for Alex Comfort gives two different titles for his third collection. The entry for Ken Smith mentions that he attended Leeds University during the time when Jon Silkin and Peter Redgrove were Gregory Fellows there. Sorry, Roger Garfitt, but an unlisted fellow presided over two years of Ken's first flowering, and Redgrove came after Ken graduated.

Finally, a point which renders this *Companion* virtually useless is the fatuous decision to give, not publishers of the books named, but the cities where those publishers are based. Imagine trying to guess which publisher is based in London!

**Bill Turner's Fables for Love *is published by Peterloo.***

## WENDY COPE

I heard Ian Hamilton being interviewed on Radio 3 about *The Oxford Companion.* The interviewer had noticed that the entry on Auden was about one and a half times as long as the one on T.S. Eliot. He asked if there had been a reassessment. Was Auden now considered the more important of the two? Hamilton explained that he had asked for the same number of words about each of them, but the man who did Auden 'went on a bit'. That isn't good enough. If you're going to let Jon Silkin look slightly more important than Charles Causley, or give Margaret Atwood (a much better novelist than poet) more space than any woman poet in Britain, it shouldn't be by accident.

A reference book should aim to be fair, rather than exciting or controversial. Most poets have, rightly, been assigned to someone who likes their work. A few, such as Craig Raine and Peter Reading, have been unlucky. Gavin Ewart gets fainter praise than he deserves.

Perhaps the worst injustice is the treatment of the Liverpool poets, dismissed as 'Beatlish ingratiators' in Hamilton's introduction, and savaged elsewhere by Martin Seymour-Smith. Henri and Patten get tiny entries to themselves. Under McGough it just says 'see Liverpool poets'. That's what you get for having hundreds of thousands of readers.

I'm glad that so many reviewers have complained about the absence of John Whitworth. Some female absentees – Kathleen Jamie, Julie O'Callaghan, Elizabeth Bartlett, Jackie Kay, Vicki Feaver – are as good as or better than some of the male poets who have been included. It reminds you of the bad old days when it was a disadvantage to be a woman. That's changing, of course. At present it is less of an advantage to be male than to speak with a northern accent. *The Oxford Companion* reflects the old unfairness rather than the fashionable kind.

Perhaps it was inevitable that a publication on this scale would be dated by the time it appeared. Even so, more effort could have been made over details – it's a while since Vikram Seth was 'best known as author of *The Golden Gate*'. That was once true, which is more than can be said for many other 'facts' presented here. Consult it with caution.

*Wendy Cope's latest collection is* **Serious Concerns (Faber).**

# JOHN OSBORNE

The strengths and weaknesses of this volume stem from the laxness of Ian Hamilton's editorial control: it is altogether more ample and inclusive than expected from a man of his stringent – no, strident – opinions; but the nearer the guide approaches the present the more gratuitous its judgements. For good or ill, the entries on poets from the first half of the century reflect current opinion (with Auden getting nine columns to Eliot's seven, Elizabeth Bishop four to MacDiarmid's two and a bit), and many are models of their kind – trenchant, knowledgeable, scrupulous. Neglected talents like Conrad Aiken, Roy Campbell, James Wright, and Anthony Hecht are judiciously assessed. And, granted the editor, the guide is surprisingly hospitable to such American experimentalists as Louis Zukofsky, Charles Olson, Frank O'Hara, and Charles Bukowski. For this reader, the best pieces in the book are those addressed to poets whose undoubted talents were in the service of ugly ideologies: Tom Paulin's defence of Ted Hughes is ablaze with passionate intelligence; whilst Clive Wilmer's essay on Ezra Pound is wonderfully poised, elegant, and persuasive.

Thereafter the book falls apart. The clearest index of this is the blatant gender bias. The brevity of the entry on Carol Ann Duffy is already, rightly, notorious. Other contemporary women poets from around the world are simply ignored: Ntzoake Shange (USA), Dinah Hawken (New Zealand), Kathleen Jamie (Scotland), Kim Morrisey (Canada). Sometimes these erasures are in offensive contrast to the treatment of men: male prose writers like John Cowper Powys, Edmund Wilson, and James Baldwin are listed because they wrote a small amount of inferior verse; but distinguished women novelists like Alice Walker and Michèle Roberts are not granted the same favour despite the fact that their poetry is far from negligible. Again, all the regional winners of the 1989 Commonwealth Poetry prize are included except the one who was a woman.

Elsewhere one remarks an eczema of errors of fact or judgement: an otherwise comprehensive entry on John Ashbery mysteriously omits his most ambitious work, *Flow Chart*; the same is true of Paul Muldoon's *Madoc*; the momentous achievements of the City Lights press go entirely unrecorded; the Robert Bly piece neglects his prose study, *Iron John*, which offers the clearest testimony to the vulgar Jungianism that undermines so much of his verse; Sylvia Plath's father did not die when she was 18; it is untrue to say that Douglas Dunn 'long worked as a librarian at the University of Hull'; references to the 'popularity' of the 'accessible' and 'unliterary' Tom Raworth are downright barmy; to say that Peter Didsbury has 'secured an academic following' is ludicrous when the sum total of academic writing on his *oeuvre* is one article; the best of the Liverpool poets, Roger McGough, is the only one not to get an entry; whilst a misprint in the Allen Curnow file would have us believe he is a woman. In short, this is a book in its penultimate draft; a book whose editor has not earned his fee; a book that is not yet worthy to carry the imprimatur of Oxford University Press.

*John Osborne is Editor of* **Bête Noire;** *he was one of the judges for New Generation Poets.*

## ROBERT CRAWFORD

The production of this book strengthens the link between poetry and marketing. Advance publicity offered many of the *Companion*able poets (ie, those no deid) the chance to buy a copy and read what had been written about them. Aware that poets not infrequently have shiny but vulnerable single-glazed egos, OUP's publicity department seized the chance to turn this to financial advantage. Publicity departments exist to help shift product, yet the structure of this book suggests that the aim from the start was to produce a controversial compromise between a *vade mecum and* a gossip shop: a volume that would generate debate in its target market. So, on the reference book side, we get names, dates, some titles, but not the sort of short primary bibliographies many readers would find useful. From time to time we're pointed towards a critical book or essay on a writer; often we ain't. In some instances we're told place of publication and/or publisher in an honest-to-God librarianly way; often these details are cavalierly absent. On the gossip side, if you're lucky, like F.T. Prince (written up by one W.G. Shepherd), you get a reverential sook; if, on the other hand, Martin Seymour-Smith writes about you, you're likely to come away limping. Younger poets, if included, tend to be treated generously, but there are unfortunate exclusions such as Kathleen Jamie.

The back of the jacket advertises star-turns, like Tom Paulin on Ted Hughes, but many of the entries are routine. The book is vulnerable to charges on grounds of gender, nation, and 'poebiz' networking, but it has more sparkle then most directories written by many hands. It's not a standard-format Oxford reference book, but it is full of information and comment, lively enough to provoke. It should have contained more plain information (lists of books, dates). Easy to criticize, hard to edit, it will zoom past its sell-by date more quickly than many A-Z's. But I'd better be honest. I bought it.

*Robert Crawford is an Editor of* Verse; *he was one of the New Generation Poets.*

## SUSHEILA NASTA

This reference collection of summaries of twentieth century 'poetries' in English makes large claims to provide a history and re-mapping of the diversity of poetry now published worldwide in the English language. The introduction clearly states the editor's intention to document and illustrate the development of and background to the evolution of modern poetics worldwide. Whilst there have been several anthologies of twentieth century poetry published over the years, this book aims to move beyond the format of the traditional biobibliographical entries and provide information on influential little magazines, movements, concepts, important formal developments and so on. This is all very laudable and on initial examination the book does seem to include a wide variety of entries from English-speaking areas other than the United Kingdom or the United States; in fact, we are told that numerically the *Companion* lists 120 poets from Australia, 110 from Canada, 60 from Africa, 40 from Asia, 35 from New Zealand and 30 from the Caribbean and includes 200 women and 100 black writers. Indeed most of the straight bibliographical entries are well written and useful on these poets but there are of course many omissions such as the important new Canadian/Trinidadian poet Marlene Nourbese Philip who has been very vocal in recent years on the whole question of language and form. More significantly whilst many literary magazines in Britain and the US are noted, there is a remarkable lack of any information on similar publications in other parts of the world, publications such as *BIM* in Barbados, *Transition* (which was first edited by Wole Soyinka) in Nigeria and so on. These publications have been critical in the development of what is now termed 'post-colonial writing'.

In fact this essentially Eurocentric attitude prevails throughout as the editor focuses specifically in his introductory discussion on what he calls the 'romance' between English and American poetry, a relationship which it seems has dominated the history of twentieth century poetry even to the extent of preventing the ex-colonies from making a 'complete break with their Anglo-American parentage'. Unfortunately this kind of 'mapping' of the terrain of modern poetry only solidifies some already fairly dubious boundaries and fails to really examine the extent to which the work for instance of the St Lucian-born Nobel Prize winner, Derek Walcott, has transformed our notions of 'insider-outsider' arguments about 'cultural purity' or how Kamau Brathwaite's innovative theories on the significance of 'nation language' in the Caribbean have been central in helping critics to re-evaluate the creative versatility of non-standard Englishes. Whilst this book appears to be doing the right things, the whole cultural orientation of the introduction fails to break down already established literary boundaries and tends to reinforce existing stereotypes of non-British or non-American writing in English. This is disappointing.

*Susheila Nasta is Editor of* Wasafiri.

## MARTYN CRUCEFIX
### *Music School*

He played pitch-dark piano for silent films.
Next day wrapped a tie around his neck
to conduct the choir through oratorios.
On Sunday the organ sang in Seaham chapel
to ease every soul out of six working days.
The blood of his family thick with music.
In those days, he and his young brother, Sam,
like Sunderland's slick wing and centre half,
had that much instinct, fiddle and ivory
drew up the stamp of working men's boots –
didn't know themselves where the next twist
would lead.  Still hit the refrain together.

Come dawn, back down their hole in the ground,
there was moleskin, snap, slapping, hollering.
He and Sam, they dreamed a school of sound
to teach kids like them to coax music out
before any soot-cough could brick it in.
But you need spirit to venture such
and the war had ripped his at the root,
though he saw no action – his twisted legs,
where props came down, saw him clear of that.
Later, years spent playing for richer men
in floating palaces between Liverpool,
New York.  For them, he made a brittle sound
to match the flutter of bank notes.

Now, white string-works show in his hands.
His skin is marked like foxing on a Bible.
'The Creation' was the last sacred work he played.
He says the darkest times were his best,
when dust motes were fireflies overhead.
The projector beam seemed a wind of light
that never ruffled a hair on anyone's head,
but blew him to gusts of music.  Never failed,
but once.  Flickering newsreel from the Front.
He sat plugging out major patriotic chords,
bent forward in praise of that great light,
when Sam was in it, above him, smiling,
puppet-waving, jerky, shin-deep in mud
where he should have been . . .
Last time he ever saw him in living flesh.
He still hears it.  How that last projector
reeled laughter out of the silence he made.

# The Elegance of the Teutonic

*Michael Hofmann on 'a man of the world and of many parts' who 'brings style to everything he does'*

**Hans Magnus Enzensberger,**
*Selected Poems,*
Translated by Hans Magnus Enzensberger &
Michael Hamburger,
Bloodaxe, £18.95 (hbk), ISBN 1 85224 290 6,
£8.95 (pbk) ISBN 1 85224 291 4

In 1979, my last year as an undergraduate, I saw Hans Magnus Enzensberger reading in the Cambridge International Poetry Festival, at the Corn Exchange (where I had heard Richard Hell and the Voidoids, and not got into Mink de Ville). I had known about him and read some of his poems, but he was probably my first experience of a live poet. He read from his own English version of his long poem *The Sinking of the Titanic*, and a little from the original German. Enzensberger was – is – Louis MacNeice's idea of a poet, not pure and pitiable (not an albatross), but a man of the world and of many parts: even more than MacNeice himself, he does other things as well, and brings style to everything he does. It was an absolutely commanding performance, an elegant man reading from his elegant poem, dressed in white and cream, for all the world as though he had just got out of one of the fabled deckchairs. (I think if Tom Wolfe had been there, he would have slunk off to change into something darker.) He looked smart, cosmopolitan and ironic (were those actually *tennis* shoes?!). He was a survivor, an *homme évadé*, celebrating in one poem and in himself the end of systems: the apotheosis of Capitalism in the *Titanic*, the Communist delusion (the ship of Cuba sinking fast even then), the Federal Republic too, as he lived *ultra vires* in the dingy liner or black iceberg of West Berlin (the datelines of *The Sinking of the Titanic* are Havana 1969–Berlin 1977). He wrote and looked as though he was through with renunciation and denial and belief, as though he had jumped off, characteristically, a little ahead of everyone else, and wanted thenceforth only wit and clarity and play.

The English version of the *Titanic* was published by Carcanet in 1981 and in paperback by Paladin in 1987 (copies still available from Carcanet, price £4.95). It remains his best book and an ideal intro-duction to his work. Since then, only prose has come out in English (the less-than-wonderful *Europe! Europe!*, a piece about immigration in *Granta*), and in Germany too he has concentrated on other things: his work as essayist, librettist, translator and publisher (the list of classic and translated titles that make up *die andere Bibliothek*). Then, a few years ago, I was given a manuscript to read: his *Selected Poems*, translated by a couple of American professors with German names. It would have come out for his sixtieth birthday, in 1989, but the translators were clowns. If ever there was a German who shouldn't sound like Gert Fröbe (or sound like Gert Fröbe looks), it is Enzensberger. The book never appeared, and I wrote to Enzensberger to express my mortification at what had happened (or my relief at what hadn't), and urged him to translate himself.

Five years later, and *wir sind soweit*. A volume of poems (with facing originals) translated partly by Michael Hamburger (his translations from the original Penguin volume of *Selected Poems* of 1968 – that series of Alvarez' – and some later things) and partly by Enzensberger himself: extrinsic pieces from the *Titanic* volume, the long poem 'The Frogs of Bikini', and most of the poems from his latest German collection, *Music of the Future* (1991). If you have German, the book offers fascinating insights into comparative translations and (that very rare thing) self-translations: Hamburger dutiful, conservative, approximate, uneasy, lopping off the last five decimal places of Enzensberger's formulations; and Enzensberger more careless, more sovereign, more opportunistic, nestling deeper into English idiom and usage, availing himself of authorial licence to render, say, in the poem 'Keeping Cool', 'Giesskanne' (watering-can) with 'toothbrush' – not as extraordinary as it may sound, both objects expressing a certain interest or stake in a medium-term future. By and large, though, Enzensberger and Hamburger are like sun and moon.

There is a side of Enzensberger that is 'Brechtian': all clarity of line and rhetoric and twists of thought, aloof from finnicky diction and that 'excessively interesting surface' that Randall Jarrell, back in the 50s, thought was a hallmark of modern poetry (see, for instance, the early poems, 'Camera Obscura' or

'Bill of Fare'). He writes international poetry like an international poet. But there is another side as well (and Brecht, ironically, had it too!) that is interested in pointless ornament, dandyism, lexical interest and surprise, the possibilities afforded by the mother tongue, the kind of things that tend to make poetry 'impossible to translate'. With Enzensberger, these things may be bits of economic or managerial or scientific jargon, the notorious German propensity for word-combinations, the wheedling mass-seduction of ad-language (at least as impossible as poetry), or they may be as beautiful and arcane as the end of 'Schwacher Trost': 'dann blüht uns/ endlich der erste Zug aus der Zigarette', where 'blüht' (generally 'blossoms', but here maybe closer to 'happens') is unexpected and almost beyond price. His own English translation (in 'Cold Comfort') is functional and no more: 'and we long/ for our first puff of smoke'.

The cavalier side of Enzensberger uses words like a gourmet chef: no ingredient is despised, anything is capable of being ennobled by its surroundings and of lending a bit of distinction: 'Stellenkegel', 'fais-moi-ça', 'Schirrmacher', 'N$^n$ sive deus', the subjunctive of 'The Frogs of Bikini', 'goldrichtig' and 'herzhaft', the poem as terminal, decadent, overbred product of civilization, 'the antennae feeling the antennae' in Rilke's phrase. But he has always – and, of late, even more – shown a puritanical side of himself too: classic modern poems on pebbles, on pubic hair, sleeping tablets, 'Old Revolution' (about Castro, I suppose):

> Wistfully the aged warrior
> scans the horizon for an aggressor.
> There is no one in sight. Even the enemy
> has forgotten about him.

He can be vigorous or delicate, teach you new words or do without (seemingly), label the things of this world like Adam, or, like a physicist-God, persuade you it almost doesn't exist. I hadn't gone back to him much these past dozen years or so. I've missed him. He's one of the greats.

**Michael Hofmann's latest collection is Corona, Corona (Faber); he was one of the 20 New Generation Poets.**

## RUTH FAINLIGHT
### *A Saga*

Cold scents the path.
Cold ores salt the caves and cliffs.
Stars sift light
through the black veil night wears,
and the sea nudges against the rocky breasts of earth.

On the weed-strewn beach
below the walls of the castle keep
she gathers bands of purple kelp
curled tight as a whip
and watches the horizon change:
Azure. Ultramarine. Indigo.

Beyond that line
where ocean plunges down the edge of the world
and the sky curdles and thickens and follows over,
each yearning to meet the other,
a high-prowed boat with russet sails is moving closer.

***Ruth Fainlight's new collection is This Time of Year (Sinclair-Stevenson, £6.99).***

# Ending up in Belfast

### by Helen Dunmore

**Carol Rumens,**
*Thinking of Skins: New & Selected Poems,*
Bloodaxe, £8.95,
ISBN I 85224 280 9

This *New & Selected* is a remarkable map of journeys. The contemporary poet can easily slip into a wandering way of life which is underpinned by residencies at one university or another, by bursaries and by travel grants. We all write our *'what I did on my paid holidays'* poems, and very irritating they can be too. An over-confident familiarity with cultures inhabited for only a few weeks or months, a splash of namedropping frilled with snatches of a foreign language which the poet does not actually speak, and an inclination towards the exotic for its own sake are just some of the pitfalls. But on the other hand there is a long and brilliant tradition of travelling poets. From Byron to Auden writers have gone abroad in order to find out who they are, as well as to experience the peculiar exhilarations of not being in Britain. It's also noticeable that some of the most acute poetic comment on British political life has come from poets who have achieved a certain distance and point of comparison through their travels. Indeed they may have travelled precisely in order to get away from a political climate which they are then able to describe without inhibition. After all, 'The Mask of Anarchy' was conceived by Shelley 'as I lay asleep In Italy.'

Carol Rumens is a poet who seems moved by profound restlessness. With her the usual attempt to pin on identifying markers does not quite work: 'born such and such a place; in such a class, religion, society, city; drawn to this or that group of contemporary poets' ... her life and her poetry would swim through the net of any such account. She is a poet who is able to saturate herself in the life of another country, without at any time losing her hold on who she is. Her attachment to eastern Europe through years of political repression was based in a practical experience which balanced what was often a deeply romantic response to particular stresses:

Oh Linden tree, oh Linden
I cannot breathe
Without your small hands, your great shade.
('Blockade')

But she has always shown herself well aware of the dangers inherent in taking on powerful experiences which are not altogether her own. She argues strongly against the viewpoint that certain issues or experiences can only be written about by those entitled in particular ways. She has chosen to open her *New & Selected* with these lines, which are unequivocal enough to amount to a statement of intent:

It was the living who took offence
At our elegies, our desire
To find out, to make amends.
They called it appropriation.
They said we were the wrong race or
religion ...
They should have asked the dead before they
judged us.
('Until We Could Hardly See Them')

At the same time she warns her readers against looking for 'my opinions about Northern Ireland' or 'any would-be objective statement about "the situation here"' in a preface to her new poems, which were largely written in Belfast. Her response to her life in Belfast is complex, vital and often edged with a very appealing sardonic humour about herself and her own life as 'a woman, English, not young'. In 'Clouding The Border', the claim she makes is large, but the homelessness of the poet, allied to her characteristic modesty, makes it ring true:

No shadow of this landscape's mine.
No stick of it estranges me.
Kavanagh sowed his hills with coin.
We share the transient legacy.

The new poems which make up the first section of the book are exciting. Rumens has found a fluidity which lets her experiment with form and voice more boldly than she has ever done. A potential weakness in her poetry has always been her reliance on a lyrical response which could become too easy, even routine. She has obviously thought about this, seen how it could limit her work, and begun to discover more pungent, startling channels of expression: 'The wind was terrorising the simple river,/Smacking the wobbly flesh about its waistband' ('St Petersburg, Reclaimed by Merchants'). The economy of this shows the length of stride Rumens is now achieving. Another new strength is a vein of expansive humour about the self and the world it discovers. Rumens has always had her astringencies, but comedy is something she has come to quite late, and with obvious relish: 'You've been fucked up and so have I, let's get fucked up some more/And take no shit from that holy cow, but show her the old barn door' ('Charm Against the Virtuous').

One of the most exciting things about being a woman poet is that there are so few models or rules about development. We just don't know what will happen when enough women get the opportunity to publish, to achieve recognition, to become known not through one collection or the odd poem but through a lifetime of work. The silencing of women's poetic voices over generations has been painful enough, but the other side of it is the current explosion of talent, energy and delight in possibilities which have never before been explored. Carol Rumens' development, from *A Strange Girl in Bright Colours* to *Thinking of Skins*, brilliantly lights up some of the possibilities. It is inspiring to see twenty years of her poetry drawn together in this *New & Selected*.

## STEVAN TONTIC

## *Trip to Paris*

Several of us so-called artists
So-called intellectuals
From so-called Bosnia & Hercegovina,
From a city in the darkened heart of this so-called civil war,
One so-called, quite fantastic day, received
An invitation from a so-called European Civil Forum
To attend a certain important meeting
In so-called France.

To leave here for Paris
would be a journey to eternity
A trip to paradise.

A seven-day wait, all present,
Problems with the so-called UN peace force
And the so-called civil authorities
Only to be informed that the trip
To so-called Europe
Had come to nothing.

Because I had been so long away from home
My wife welcomed me as if I had
Really been on a long journey;
She – the only one not so-called –
was almost ashamed in case the neighbours found out
I had so quickly and with such disdain, left Paris
To return to this place of unavoidable death.

**(Translated from the Serbian by Mary Radosavljevi)**

# A Twentieth Century Book of the Dead

*Ken Smith on a volume bearing witness to the most bloody century*

**Against Forgetting,**
Edited by Carolyn Forché,
W.W. Norton, $19.95,
ISBN 0 393 30976 2

The title is from Apollinaire's *Stanzas Against Forgetting*. At nearly 800 pages by 145 poets this is a mammoth anthology of what its editor Carolyn Forché terms 'the poetry of witness': poetry that has risen out of the sufferings and traumas of our century: 'poem as trace, poem as evidence', poetry that has come of war and repression. It begins with the Armenian genocide when between 1909 and 1918 some 1.5 million Armenians were murdered by the Ottoman Turks. From there the trail of tears runs through World Wars I and II, the Spanish Civil War, the Holocaust or *Shoah*, through Soviet tyranny in Russia and Eastern Europe, war and struggle in the Middle East, Africa and South America, wars in India and Pakistan, in Korea and Vietnam, the struggle for civil liberties in the United States, to the sufferings of China culminating in Tiananmen Square in 1989.

Such a catalogue of misery is sadly mundane, and indeed incomplete, as the Balkan wars make clear. Such poetry as has come out of these extreme conditions is miraculous, a testimony to hope and to the future, for to write is to wish to be read and understood. And yet it should not surprise us that extremity squeezes out poetry in response to itself. All the work here is by poets who were in some way involved, who have themselves been in prisons or camps, victims of exile, censorship, persecution, torture or murder, or who fought in wars or in resistance to dictatorships and occupations. For the most part they are poets 'for whom the normative processes of the nation-state have failed' (Forché). The other criteria for inclusion are that the poets must have been recognized as significant within their own literatures, and their work available either in English or in translation. These are necessary limitations. Eight years in the making, this is a selection of the work available – about a quarter of what Forché collected, though as an anthology it is already too big and too unwieldy.

That this is so is not because there are too many poets, but too many poems by many of the poets included, and far too many long poems. To my mind the shorter the poem, the more telling. There are some doubtful inclusions, and too many Americans as to render the collection ethnocentric. Gertrude Stein in occupied France was surely a remoter witness than any Radnoti, Desnos, or Eluard. Pound's inclusion (*Pisan Canto LXXIV*) as a 'witness' is contentious. Forché has not enough resisted the pressures and temptations to include big names at the expense of those who merely live and die. Zbigniew Herbert has written more biting ironies than here on the hypocrisies of the all powerful, and there are Różewicz poems more apposite to postwar Poland. The attack on the guilty, on those responsible for all this misery, seems often blunted. And there are lamentable exclusions: Ungaretti, Sorescu, and because there is a section on the Spanish War ending in 1939, but nothing of the long Franco night that followed it, there's no Blas de Otero ('*here we say, If there is no bread, sticks will do*'). Attila Jozsef appears in the section on Repression in Eastern and Central Europe (1945-91) when he jumped to his death on a railway line in Szarszo in 1937. Such are the vagaries of classification. There's nothing of Ulster, no Portugal, no Indonesia. We have Neruda and Vallejo, but no Paz. And from South East Asia we have only the witness of Westerners, mostly Americans who participated, but no balance of Vietnamese. Surely? At the book's beginnings poems are accompanied by dates, but all too soon this useful notation discontinues. In an anthology of personal experience, dates would be useful, providing a historic context for the individual poem. Introductory biographic notes are often too brief: Mahmoud Darwish's 'We Travel Like Other People' would mean more were we told that it was written after the PLO and the Palestinians had been expelled from Beirut by the Israelis in 1982; he did not merely 'return to Galilee' as if it were a career decision, and knowing this the poem would be more poignant: 'We have a country of words. Speak Speak so we may know the end of this travel'. As for Bobrowski, born in Tilsit 'now on the border of Germany and Lithuania', I doubt the Poles would agree.

That said, this remains an invaluable collection that parallels the technologies of terror that have developed, in this century, industrialized murder, increasingly efficient repression, and distanced the soldier from his target while increasingly targetting the civilian. There are moving and brilliant poems here, deploying much irony, many of them born of the act of piecing together fragments, of reconstructing the language brutalized by politics, as witness Milosz: 'Man constructs poetry out of the names found in ruins'; Radnoti's 'Picture Postcards', Günter Eich's 'Old Postcards'; Grass's ear at the phone listening 'to the new tone for busy'; Levi's 'struggling sense into a senseless message'; Erich Fried's definition of a 'Safety detonator/is a peasant tied to a rope/and driven across a minefield'; Nicanor Parra's 'The poet's duty is this:/To improve on the blank page'.

The poet improves on the page as witness, through affirmation and solidarity, rebuilding the instrument of language and redefining a role in so doing. There are great treasures of the human spirit here, great affirmations and great denials, where (*pace* Adorno, *gratis* Levi) not to write after Auschwitz is to let the bloody barbarians win. 'Even if I had been there/I could not have told their story', says Ariel Dorfman: 'Let them speak for themselves'. And Quasimodo: 'life is here/in every No that seems a certainty'. And there is this, by Dan Pagis, who escaped in 1944 after three years in a concentration camp:

'Written in Pencil in the Sealed Railway Car'

here in this carload
i am eve
with abel my son

if you see my other son
cain son of man
tell him that i

---

Ken Smith is the editor, with Judi Benson, of *Klaonica: Poems for Bosnia* (Bloodaxe, £7.95); his latest collection is *Tender to the Queen of Spain* (Bloodaxe, £6.95).

## PETER WYLES
### *Aspects of the President*

President, playing the saxophone, hoping to be liked.
Hilary is hectoring the doctors, Chelsea
practices the pianola, her father's tunes.
The press are sniffing underwear in the bathroom
and Socks the cat is ripping up the platform.
– This is Washington Mr President.

President, jogging in the park, eating grease
at Arkansas Bill's Big Fat Roosters.
President, smoking dope but not inhaling,
dodging and weaving. Today the zigzag,
tomorrow the sidewalk. 'Change my mind?
Love to.  Tomorrow at  five?  Certainly.'

President, in high heels and a garter-belt,
waggling his fat butt in Times Square,
watching the polls, sniffing the Wall St Journal,
but never inhaling, he never inhales.
President, next to his heart, a jackass,
embroidered on his boxer shorts, a weathercock.

## JAMES A. DAVIES
### *Revisiting*

We moved in but the neighbours didn't call;
I knew their chance would never come again.
Sometimes we saw them near our garden wall;
my mother stared in anger, then disdain.

Two old sisters; they never spoke to us
but moved among the beds in gloves and hats.
They made few sounds, no geriatric fuss
flustered the lawns or chased away the cats.

Their old gardener hovered – we'd paid him off –
to mow the grass and lop the heavy trees.
They gave him tasks until they'd said enough,
then, sunned, doffed hats, peeled gloves, sipped fingered teas

in their elegant summerhouse; china,
white-blue, tinkled; grass green to the very
door. Luminous, embalmed Edwardiana
lingering in hierarchical ease.

And then they left; the gardener went away.
We never knew what brought things to a close.
The dark house glowered through each empty day,
the lawns grew rough, weeds strangled every rose.

One evening, aged fourteen, I climbed the wall
as autumn drizzle bowed the dripping trees.
Windows blazed with renovators' lights. All
sisterly presence long gone with the breeze

that swung the summerhouse door. Its cracked glass
filtered smeared beams on cushions dark with rain,
leaves shifted on the once-scrubbed floor where grass
pushed past the sisters' ghostly steps. Two cane

chairs
      fallen flat
               where all my life I've seen
two dying ladies view ordered beauty
through translucent cups.
                        Thick, blurred boughs lean
darkly.
      Mother's world of form and duty,
fiercely departed.

Beyond soft walls I hear the wild machine,

# A Poet more than Himself

*John Bayley on a writer who dreams of equilibrium and good order*

**Douglas Dunn,**
*Dante's Drum-Kit,*
Faber, £6.99,
ISBN 0 571 170552
***Reading Douglas Dunn,***
Eds. Robert Crawford and David Kinloch,
Edinburgh University Press, £14.95 hbk,
ISBN 0 7486 0369 7

***Douglas Dunn by Gerald Mangan***

**A** study could be written on the detachment, indeed the alienation, of the kind of poetry in the last 150 years or so which has made a real and significant impact upon the consciousness of its time. No more great committed romantics, Shelleys, Byrons, Petofis, even the Goethes and the Wordsworths. Instead, poets like Baudelaire and Leopardi, Emerson, Whitman, Tennyson, Browning, whose effect on their reading public was in time no less influential, but who always stood a significant distance outside society, who had no choice but to remain their own men. And this phenomenon was increased and strengthened by the coming of Modernism. Cavafy and Pound, *The Waste Land*, how essentially solitary they are, how much voices crying in the wilderness! Eliot may strive to integrate himself with a vision of the Christian society, or the young Auden with Marxism, but no true poetry reader is deceived. Eliot remains his strange lonely self; Auden the marvellously light-hearted and irresponsible creator of a world of coming doom and present gaiety, a world created entirely by himself.

And this essential selfness or selfhood is the hallmark of post-romantic poetry. Outside me, no salvation: the old slogan of the Church fits the case sardonically well. Look at Lowell and Berryman. Look at Larkin. He is now abused for his 'views': but every poetry reader knows that they don't matter a damn: that Larkin was a great poet because he was his own man and nothing else. It is a singular and curious modern phenomenon, and one that most people naturally don't like. Some Hardyan Ironic Spirit seems to whisper: can a politically correct poet be saved? Or at least a poet who strives to be politically correct in his poetry.

Of course he can be, but at some unspecifiable and unquantifiable cost. The case of Douglas Dunn

is particularly interesting here, because he is an admirable poet – really good – and yet every line, every word he writes breathes not only a natural goodness of the spirit, but a kind of unmistakable civic virtue, what he has himself described in an interview with John Haffenden as: 'an aspiration towards justice, a dream of equilibrium, good order, benevolence, love, of the kind of sanity which men have it within their means to create'. That might be Shelley speaking in one of his Prefaces, but Shelley would be writing 'Adonais' or 'Prometheus Unbound', not about Terry Street. One of the liveliest poems in this very much alive collection, 'Audenesques for 1960', is not only true and touching about all this, but twinkles with Dunn's special kind of shrewdness.

Neither very brave, nor very beautiful,
Nor heterosexually inclined, but still, you were,

My imagination's mentor, fantasy's ear
Attentive as I twaddled half-baked poetical
                                    opinions
Walking to work in Renfrew County Library.

You had become one of your doting readers
Before death claimed you in shadowy Vienna.
You, too, were a way of happening.

Auden, as Dunn, says, 'helped to populate my private madness'; and yet Dunn grew up in his craft as a naturally committed poet, one for whom society as it was existed; and not, like Auden, a poet who populated his own private world. How paradoxical these things about poetry are, or have become. For it is the poet as self who feeds us and our dreams in the fractured world of today, not the poet who aspires, as Dante did (Dunn's title is significant) towards a dream of equilibrium and good order.

Dunn's sturdy, naturally civic character must come in some degree from identification with his own country, Scotland, just as Heaney's comes from a similar identification with Ireland. The mere English poet, Larkin, had no native identity in this sense. The long poem, 'Dressed to Kill', which ends *Dante's Drum-Kit*, makes the best possible use of a national sense and sentiment, which is quite disenchanted and yet absolutely sterling into the bargain. (No pun intended, though it was originally commissioned by the BBC for a Film Programme shot at Stirling Castle.) It is an altogether splendid poem, and Larkin would have revelled in it, though he could not himself have done anything like it (he was uneasy when he *tried* to be English). It reads like a quick march with the band and must have been really grand on a sound-track. Its epigraph is from James Wright: 'When I was a boy/ I loved my country', and it ends in the mad gaiety of the imagined battle – 'This painting's an heroic thrill/ That stirs my blood, and always will', even though 'The patriotic puddle's a sink/Where racial monster's come to drink'.

The Thin Red Line above a mantelpiece
Defeats my pacificisms and strikes me dumb –
The glory that was kilt and riflegrease,
The grandeur that was bayonet and rum.

Poe's lines about the glory that was Greece and the grandeur that was Rome are made just the right use of: the irony conterpointing the tension between excitement and sanity, reason and the wild instinct that 'always will'. A really fine and spirited poem. But *Dante's Drum-Kit* contains many that are as good. 'Disenchantments' is Dunn at his most

thoughtful, though in a sense at his least convincing; but the honesty in its lines is that of the real Maker, and it earns the line that ends it: 'Look to the living, love them, and hold on'. 'Just Standing There' and 'Poor People's Cafés' are tough and memorable in another sense, finely and strongly made. How right Dunn was to protest against Malcolm Bradbury's claim that 'writing is the trade and criticism the profession' (suitably equivocal as it is) by counter-claiming that 'writing is an art, and criticism the function of its curators'.

That comment is quoted in *Reading Douglas Dunn*, a first-rate collection of essays on the poet, which belongs to a solid and indispensable series (Modern Scottish Writers) put out by Edinburgh University Press. It comes in Richard Price's very good and challenging essay on Dunn's criticism, and its general relation to Scottish poetry. Equally good are Glyn Maxwell on 'Dunn, Larkin and Decency', a thought-provoking topic, and Ian Gregson on 'There are many worlds', that truth of the imagination that Dunn found with Larkin, and which gives its unique mixture of uprightness and honesty to the tones of his poetry.

**John Bayley has recently published his second novel, *Alice* (Duckworth, £14.99).**

# Fine Tuning

## by Conor Kelly

**John Montague,**
*Time in Armagh*,
The Gallery Press, £5.95,
ISBN 1 85235 112 8
**Dennis O'Driscoll,**
*Long Short Story*,
Anvil, £7.95,
ISBN 0 85646 256 X
**Gerard Fanning,**
*Easter Snow*,
Dedalus, £4.95,
ISBN 1 873790 15 5

In Ireland poetry is different. As Marianne Moore put it in 'Spenser's Ireland' – 'Every name is a tune'. Perhaps as a result of a colonial heritage, perhaps as a result of a dual tradition, perhaps as a result of an official yet under-utilized national language, the Irish poet is often more attuned to the suasions between poem and place, sound and social background, tonality and townland than his British counterpart. Metre and prosody are still vital and energetic features of the contemporary landscape of Irish poetry. And the three poets under review, however diverse they may be in their linguistic and social concerns, still manifest the benefits of playing a local melody in tune.

## John Montague

'I do not think I could exaggerate the harshness of our schooldays'. That sentence from the preface to *Time in Armagh*, John Montague's account of the five teenage years he spent in St Patrick's College, a junior seminary in the ecclesiastical capital of Ireland, brings us into a world familiar to readers of Irish literature: a world of sadistic celibate teachers instilling brutality, fear, guilt and shame in their young charges. Interspersed with short prose pieces, this unified sequence of 21 poems is an unashamedly autobiographical portrait of the poet as potential for the priesthood. Sent at the age of twelve

from the home where he was 'reared by long-suffering aunts' – his family history is eloquently and emotionally explored in his best collection, *The Dead Kingdom* – Montague was to spend his formative years as a 'sensitive plant' in the all-male, anti-female community of what he calls a 'typical Catholic boarding school education'.

The book is dominated by the guilt absorbed in the bloodstream of these boarded boys. 'In an age when tenderness was needed, we got none'. They got instead, a sense of their own bodies as instruments of sin.

> The confessor's crouched ear, raised palm:
> 'Did you draw fluids from your body again?'
> A heavy sigh: 'Madness grows from self-
> pollution.'
> The warm, vague seawash of absolution.

The rhyme registers the distance the poems attempt to traverse from the pollution of the priestly mentors to the absolution of passionate poetry. (Montague was to grow up to become one of Ireland's most erotic poets.)

And that pollution was endemic. 'I do not blame the priests for this, for whom we were God-fodder, nor my classmates, because we all had to survive'. But while the poems may not assign blame, they skilfully chart the pain of such pollution. And the ironies of their educational inadequacies are starkly revealed, as in the case of the nicknamed 'Father Kangeroo':

> Our lean bespectacled Australian Classics
> master
> Made us insert a blank sheet of paper
> Over the reproduction of naked statues
> In our slim *Daily Life in Ancient Rome*,
> – thus drawing our sniggering attention to
> them.

The harshness of the life is counterpointed by the lightness of the poem. Montague is aware that that harshness was not incidental or accidental: 'this is your old-style Catholic schooling, way back to medieval times'. Hence 'a free style is out of the question'.' It is one of the great merits of this slim but absorbing study that the discipline of the schooling is reflected in the discipline of the poems:

> This low-pitched style seeks exactness,
> Daring not to betray the event.

There is hope and humour and honesty in these pages. The education took place against the background of a changing world dominated by the Second World War. German planes flew low over the school, German prisoners were observed in a nearby prisoner-of-war camp and newsreels at the local cinemas brought the horrors of the modern world to 'our parochial brand of innocence'. But it was a parochial world of brutal innocence and one that soon gave way to the complexities of a modern troubled Ireland in which John Montague was to play a significant part, putting the conflicting politics in tune.

## Dennis O'Driscoll

A more prosaic music is evident in the poems of Dennis O'Driscoll, where the sparse deflationary style owes much to the work of Eastern-European poets whose merits he has often proclaimed in the pages of *Poetry Review*. Here the conversations of the shopping aisles is more evident than the whispered intimacies of the confessional. Yet the book is full of echoes of other modes and other tunes. O'Driscoll can take Robert Frost's 'The Road Not Taken' and, paring back the rhythms, rhymes and cadences, deconstruct it to a deliberately downbeat version of itself.

How tantalising they are,
those roads you glimpse
from car or train,
bisected by a crest
of grass perhaps,
keeping their
destinations quiet.

You remember a brimming
sea on the horizon
or an arch of trees
in reveries of light;
then a bend that cut
your vision off
abruptly!

Some day you must return
to find out how they end.

There are many roads traversed in *Long Short Story* and most of them, while unnamed, have their own little airs: wry, dispassionate bagatelles. The language and the rhythms are tuned to a distinctly modern landscape of hatchbacks, term-loans, layoffs, rush-hour delays, Sunday papers, January sales, smokeless fuel, Chinese takeaways, DIY shops, suburban shopping malls and methodical office procedures. It is a world ignored in much contemporary poetry, yet here it is not so much celebrated as calibrated. At their best, and there are many successes in this generous collection, language and landscape merge as every name – brand-names included – is tuned. The poems may be sparse, but they are suitably sparse.

Efforts to expand the range of these poems with lush diction ('Fruit Salad') or intensified imagery ('Rose Windows') are not convincing. Far better is the manner in which the material world is counterpointed by a constant recognition of how and where all roads end – in death. There are taut poems on cancer sufferers ('It is easier to prove the existence / of leukaemia than of God'), accident cases ('Case Studies'), terrorist victims ('Irish Cuttings' and 'Mistaken Identity') and terminal diseases (passim). The shadow of a personal grief – there are poems about the deaths of his parents – sighs in the margins. But what gives these poems, and this book, a subtle understated strength is a cool, faintly ironic tone finding itself in tune.

## Gerard Fanning

Another tone, another set of tunes. The poems in Gerard Fanning's first collection *Easter Snow* are also concerned with naming, but in a tentative exploratory fashion like a cartographer annotating inhospitable territory.

I try, as I can, to understand
these wintry acres –
a soldier's nightmare of no cover,
looted trucks cradling the ditches as
mild corrosions burn the moon-white fields.

The mild corrosions of modern life meeting a mutable landscape is the subject of these delicately spun poems. The voice is constantly changing pitch, adapting itself to new and wider perspectives as the poems navigate their quiet way:

a tired odyssey in a world
grown warm with our cold grip.

This, the voice of a German bomber pilot over Belfast in 1941, is one of many voices, tentatively and often tremulously seeking warmth in a cold world, and seeking it in tune. This book, winner both of the Brendan Behan Award for a best first collection and of the 1993 Rooney Prize for Irish Literature, is an assured and auspicious debut.

## MARTIN MOONEY

# *Two Pages from A Travel Diary*

**I**

I'm no sooner home than I'm away again, she says,
I hardly see her, though she hardly changes.
I know I'll be with her again days in advance
when every woman in the airport looks like she does

and I squirm on the plane to hide my erection.
This is love, carrying her photograph everywhere
and calling at all hours, long distance. Love
and timezones, someone should write a book about it.

The Harbour airport, then a taxi straight to bed.
'You're no sooner home,' she says, and then comes
out with it: 'How does it feel to make love
with a pregnant woman?' Imagine getting the word

like that, just as you're catching your breath,
till it sinks in like acceleration, take-off's
slap of pressure in your ears as the plane
climbs, and home becomes a tiny plan of itself.


**II**

A stewardess translates the safety manual
into semaphore – give her two paddles and she might
be guiding bombers onto a carrier deck.
The darkened cabin has its own runway lights.

The fuselage quivers like a nervous wreck
as, seat-belted, I brood on what you've told me.
It's as frightening and energising as bad weather.
I tour its implications like a foreign country.

Everything has its counterparts and miniatures –
the engines kick alive, I wince and grin;
months before impact, your minute passenger
is already folded into the crash position.


*Martin Mooney's first collection, Grub, (Blackstaff, £5.95) was
awarded the Brendan Behan Memorial Award for 1994.*

## Playing to the Gallery

### by Dannie Abse

Paul Durcan,
*Give Me Your Hand*,
Macmillan, £9.99,
ISBN 0333 585 93 3

**D**uring the 1950s the middle-brow *Spectator* spokesmen of the Movement poets delighted in deflating cultural pretentiousness. 'Filthy Mozart' might have been a joke cry but the Movement's sincere suspicions of High Culture led a number of them to pose as outrageous Philistines. Among their anti-cultural interdictions, 'No more poems about paintings' seemed to have point since so many inert post-war pieces about sculpture and paintings had been published. There were other arguments offered elsewhere. The American poet, James Merrill, declared in 1960, 'I'm somewhat prejudiced against poems written about existing works of art. A certain parasitism is involved, I'm afraid: riding on someone else's coat-tails. Not that there aren't some beautiful ones ...'

With galleries being increasingly visited by the general public, travel abroad more commonplace, and the ubiquitousness of colour reproductions, not a few 20th century poets have indeed contributed 'beautiful ones'. In 1986, when I was privileged to co-edit *Voices in the Gallery*, sponsored by the Tate, we were able to include eighty such poems, chosen from literally thousands of 20th century poems about paintings. We eschewed poems that were purely 'parasitical' and merely descriptive but chose those where the painting was *experienced* by the poet, inhabited by the poet, and thus survived the distance from their source: poems in their own right. However, we trusted that with the adjacency of poem and picture an illuminating synergy would result to allow serious entertainment for the reader, if not by setting his/her imagination free, then at least by temporarily and profitably confining it.

Now the National Gallery has sponsored a similarly elegant book, having commissioned the quirky, talented Irish poet, Paul Durcan, to write about 50 of their paintings. Interesting as some of these poems are, few of them would survive the distance from their source. One that does so is 'Portrait of a Lady in Yellow'. Here Durcan imagines that a profile portrait of a young woman by Baldovinetti represents a victim of an IRA explosion in a Charing Cross Road bookshop. The father (mother?) has been summoned to London to identify the daughter and the poem itself is a monologue by the parent. I am reminded of the great lament by the 15th century Welsh poet, Lewis Glyn Cothi for his dead son. Cothi wrote: 'The death of Sion stands by me/ Stabbing me twice in the chest./My boy, my twirling taper,/My bosom, my heart, my song,/My prime concern till my death,/My clever bard, my daydream,/My toy he was, my candle/My fair soul, my one deceit ...' Durcan writes:

O my daughter.
My mandolin in the window.
My bedroom door.
My ikon.
My handkerchief under my pillow.
My snake.
Three feminine vowels.
I miss you.

Most of the poems lack this serious tone and aspire to be humorously vernacular. When Paul Durcan does not self-indulgently divagate too much from the subject of the painting, when he keeps to the wit of brevity, then his humour which so often depends on the aggression of satire – 'taking the piss' – allows the reader to chuckle genuinely instead of groan as one does after an unfunny joke or a pun. Alas, for the most part Durcan presents himself as the Dave Allen of Poets who, like that Irish comedian, delights in funny blasphemy. Nothing wrong with that; nothing wrong with spouting monologues with inveterate flippancy, providing you don't happen to have a reverence for a particular painting, if not for theological dogma.

Though there are occasions when one might wish to salute the wildness of Durcan's inventive fancy, one is too often aware that these cabaret performances, monologues spoken by characters in the pictures, allow an untutored reader to opine that modern poetry is just prose cut up into arbitrary line-lengths. I take at random a half dozen lines. Durcan ventriloquizes for Jesus:

Mother was comprehensively insignificant
In the scheme of things in Belfast city.
She had no position on or in anything
Nor did she read newspapers

Except the odd tabloid or watch TV
Except for *Coronation Street* ...

Why are these undistinguished lines not continuous? Why do the lines begin with the presumption of capital letters? The above passage is not atypical.

Sophisticated readers, irrespective of whether the monologues are prose or poetry, will protest that trawling through most of this book is like being in an art gallery with an anecdotal companion manically trying to be funny. Worse, that as one looks at a painting long known and admired one's vision is soiled by the flippancy of a too proximate chatterbox. I felt like that when I turned the page to a reproduction of Rubens's 'Samson and Delilah', a painting I've long thought to be wonderful . In it Samson is asleep on Delilah's richly brocaded lap and a Philistine is cutting Samson's hair. Durcan gives the 'barber' these lines about Delilah:

She whispers to me: He make the big love.
I whisper: He what?
She whispers: He make the big love ...
She whispers: He do the whole intercourse
Not just middle
But beginning end middle ...

And so on. Somehow, because I revere the painting I resent the cheap tone of the 'barber's' monologue. I resent, too, that Durcan's poems rarely pay true homage to the painting he writes about, unlike so many of the 'beautiful ones' of our best 20th century poets. On the other hand, it should be remembered that these monologues are all commissioned – and commissioned poetry, even by gifted poets, as one knows from the lamentable efforts of successive poets laureate, is only occasionally memorable.

**Dannie Abse's *Selected Poems* was recently published by Penguin, price £6.99.**

## MAURICE RIORDAN
### *L. S. Lowry's Man Lying on a Wall*
**(after Michael Longley)**

I'm asleep, you say, possibly dead.
I sleep then with my mouth closed
on a cigarette, with one eye open
to watch its delicate tower of ash.
That explains the stiff expression,
though not the pink buttonhole
or squashed bowler, blue cravat,
the suggestive spire my hands make,
the size fourteen shoes – nor the fact
I've one foot stretched on cool brick,
the other in perspective's mid-air . . .

Have another look at these bricks:
no two are the exact same shape
or shade of municipal brown.
Each one was drawn, or laid,
so you can see how the wall rose,
level and true, to carry me off
(a tramp or executive?) half-way
from pavement to the sky,
while you edge closer in the queue.

**Maurice Riordan's first collection, A Word from the Loki, is forthcoming from Faber.**

# Crisis? This Crisis

## by David Wheatley

*A Rage for Order:*
*Poetry of the Northern Ireland Troubles,*
Edited by Frank Ormsby,
Blackstaff Press, £12.95, ISBN0 85640 490 X
*The Chosen Ground: Essays on the*
*Contemporary Poetry of Northern Ireland,*
Edited by Neil Corcoran,
Seren, £8.95, ISBN 1 85411 028 4

**T**he danger is in the eloquence of the discretions. As Beckett's Unnamable puts it: 'it is all very fine to keep silence, but one also has to consider the kind of silence one keeps' – exile and cunning please copy! Not that the poems in Frank Ormsby's *A Rage for Order: Poetry of the Northern Ireland Troubles* haven't been given good cause to perfect all three habits. For the writer used to confronting 'the thing not done, the atrocity', in Hugh Maxton's forked phrase (is that one 'thing' or two?), hearing oneself not breaking the silence has come to seem all too like a part of the act, the urge to weigh up one's 'responsible *tristia*' all too like a genteel scalpel and compress for the crimes of omission by which the other sort are daily underwritten. 'While you do what? Write rondeaux?' Whatever the answer to that question, one demurs at letting Muldoon's Pancho Villa ('Co-author of such volumes/ As *Blood on the Rose,/The Dream and the Drums/* And *How It Happened Here*') take all the credit for having asked it. Ormsby's poets certainly do.

Michael Longley admits that the poet would be 'inhuman not to respond' but 'a poor artist if he did not seek to endorse that response imaginatively', Seamus Heaney demands a poetry able to 'encompass the perspectives of humane reason' without sacrificing 'the religious intensity of the violence [in] its deplorable authenticity and complexity', while Seamus Deane is troubled by the thought that an Irish artist can be 'more troubled by the idea that they should be troubled by a crisis than they are by the crisis itself'. In refusing to restrict the definition of what a 'Troubles' poem is to the realms of the 'depressingly instructive', Ormsby has been able to assemble an impressively free-wheeling rebuke to the imperatives of 'instant politics' in the historical scope of his selections – Heaney's 'Casualty' rubs shoulders with a *Cure at Troy* extract, Longley's 'Wreaths' with his versions of Tibullus and Homer, Mahon's eponymous 'Rage for Order' and 'Afterlives' with 'Courtyards in Delft' (with its last verse rescued from the 'Maenads' of Mahon's self-editing), Tom Paulin's 'And where do you stand on the national question?' with his version of Pushkin's 'To Chaadaeff'. Similarly, the love poem, with its unapologetic submission of statutory 'Act(s) of Union' to the more fleshly kind, would seem an unlikely or irresponsible vehicle for comment on the Northern *imbroglio*. It is only poetic justice then that some of the most searing contributions to *A Rage for Order* address themselves to just this topic – Heaney's 'Act of Union' itself, Durcan's 'Ireland 1972,' John Montague's 'Cave', or Longley's hankering in his verse letter to James Simmons

> To exercise in metaphor
> Our knockings at the basement door,
> A ramrod mounted to invade
> The vulva, Hades' palisade,
> The Gates of Horn and Ivory
> Or the walls of Londonderry.

– the ironists's tongue for once being firmly stuck in somebody's else cheek. As one would expect, the greater part of these poems were written in or in exile of one sort or another from post-1968 Northern Ireland; but room is also found for the longer historical views of Kipling's 'Ulster 1912', generous swathes of Hewitt and MacNeice, Donald Davie's 'Belfast on A Sunday Afternoon', and Larkin's 'The Importance of Elsewhere', with more recent contributions from Tony Harrison, Iain Crichton Smith, Fleur Adcock, Joseph Brodsky and Yevtushenko all adding an international *vigor mortis* to the 'dying art' with which this anthology answers history's 'dreary epics/ of the muscle-bound'.

The essays which Neil Corcoran has assembled in *The Chosen Ground* also emphasize dislocation and exile, albeit with an accompanying commitment to the identity of a specifically Northern experience of these conditions. Accordingly, the largely journalistic entity that Thomas Kinsella sees in the 'Northern Ireland Renaissance' in *The New Oxford Book of Irish Verse* – to take one well-known dissenting voice, conspicuous in his absence from *A Rage for Order* – receive short shrift from a volume adamant in its insistence that Northern Irish poetry demands recognition on terms which neither Kinsella on the one side nor the *Penguin Book of Contemporary British Poetry* on the other is willing to give it. In the lengthiest and most magisterial of these essays, John Kerrigan's 'Ulster Ovids', the

Latin poet is taken as a touchstone for the polymorphous quality of Northern writing – from Mahon's *Tristia*-tinged 'Ovid in Tomis' to his versions from the *Amores* or the *Metamorphoses*-like *Sweeney Astray* or 'Immram' (from Muldoon's *Why Brownlee Left*) – in the tradition of anti-imperialist paraphrase launched by Pound's *Homage to Sextus Propertius*. In her excellent piece on Muldoon and 'The Lie of the Land', Clair Wills takes up the same argument in an exploration of the border-transactions between classical mythopoeia and postmodern farce in *Meeting the British*, which she imaginatively aligns with the theme of skewed commercial exchange on which that volume dwells so extensively. Other essays on individual poets include Thomas Docherty's annotations on the 'Initiations, Tempers, Seductions' of a Medbh McGuckian, the slipperiness of whose postmodernism (on this reading) may be one reason for her having eluded Ormsby's grip in *A Rage for Order*, Gerald Dawe on Montague, Bernard O'Donoghue on Tom Paulin, and an essay on 'Bog Poems and Book Poems' by Richard Brown moving effortlessly from the Ulster of 'Armoured cars and tanks and guns' to the 'self-generating, self-consuming postmodern Switzerland of the pun'. What would Pancho Villa think of it all?

---

David Wheatley is a poet and critic; he features in the forthcoming *After Ovid: New Metamorphoses* (Faber).

## MARY O'DONNELL
### *At the Zoological Gardens*

The smell is part of the reason I return.
  I have always come, alone, or with a lover,
once newly-married, learnt early to avoid
  the Sunday empire of ice-cream and Coke.
Again, upwind, I catch the feline funk,
  a sullen whiff of cattish viscera,
all that is dispassionate and wild.
  Before the piebald Colobus Monkeys,
buggy-pushing mothers point, explain.
  An Arctic wind is blowing now in May,
  but lonely lovers do not stay away.

Two hippopotami glisten in mud,
  their grave, aquatic feet engulfed and slurping,
as if to siphon subterranean ales.
  Intent on exercise, I face the wind,
scoot the buggy past a sombre couple,
  past soigné Jaguars (ignored by my child,
who points a rhetorical finger at a sparrow).
  Again, all that is dispassionate and wild;
downwind, I breathe the fug of warm cat flesh.
  An Arctic wind is blowing now in May,
  but lonely lovers do not stay away.

Punk madonna and infant, orangutans
  embrace and snuggle deep; behind a grille,
a sociable black pig snorts: children  shriek,
  make retching sounds then speak of shit and filth.
Polar Bears slouch to the shape of bean-bags,
  coal eyes senile, Sea Lions bask in a pool,

bark and snigger at the trippers out from school.
   Everywhere, the shivering shrubs, women
in anoraks; and now my child asleep.
   An Arctic wind is blowing now in May,
   but hungry lovers dare not stay away.

A topography of foulest primal moments
   (reviled by thinking people in the know),
nobody here on weekdays but natives
   from a one-sexed continent, let loose
with others of the species.  The women
   play Mummy, the children – vague, hysterical
or sleeping, converge at last on a place
   of beautiful, wasted creatures,
bored, their essences squandered for all time.
   Lost forever to Arctic winds in May,
   lovers and loveless do not stay away.

*Mary O'Donnell's first collection,* **Reading the Sunflowers,** *was published by Salmon in 1990.*

## JUSTIN QUINN
### *Questions*

One leaf, this moment gone,
Let go the branch and started failing.
The nearby roof was reddish brown
And nothing other.  All along
It, fluttering, asking, a shadow ran.

What or who arranged all this?
Is this impromptu or pure event,
These cadenced questions, slates, and shadows,
And is there love? What shape or movement
Has it? Does it fall or hold us?

Who'd think these questions of great import
To the nation or the status quo?
Clouds or clear skies high apart
From slate and leaf and branch below.
Shadows happen or don't, in short.

But there is more to this that defeats
Your eye.  Question marks like sickles
Come ripping up the roofs and streets,
And you gaze up into weather, at a loss
To know who loves, who asks, who hates.

*A selection of Justin Quinn's work appears in* **New Poetries,** *edited by Michael Schmidt (Carcanet £8.95).*

# Our Irish Correspondent

## by Conor Kelly

**Ciaran Carson,**
*First Language,*
Gallery, £5.95,
ISBN 1 85235 128 4

**'C**oncatenated words from which the sense seemed gone ...' That eloquent and elegiac line which never made it past Ezra Pound's editorializing into the final version of *The Waste Land* could provide an apt epigraph for the winner of the 1993 T.S. Eliot prize for poetry – Ciaran Carson's *First Language*. Yet the uses to which the Irish poet's concatenated words are put are as different as late-19th century Boston is from late-20th century Belfast. If Eliot reputedly saw his modernist epic as 'just a piece of rhythmical grumbling', Carson presents his hyperactive collocation of poems as a cacophony of rhythmical explosions, 'auxiliarizing verse with prose'. If Eliot gathered his gloom into a mosaic of quotations ('These fragments I have shored against my ruin'), Carson excitedly burrows among the rubble of an exploded language, rebuilding the fragments into a glorious tower of words.

The beautifully designed cover of this, Carson's fourth collection, is a reproduction of a painting of the Tower of Babel. It is an apt image for a book in which the multiplicity and munificence of language is not only celebrated but detonated with an explosive vigour. London Bridge may be falling down repeatedly in *The Waste Land*, but in Carson's Belfast the tower of Babel is repeatedly exploding in language. 'My Babel-babble', he calls it in one poem; 'a verdurous babble' in another; and everything is caught up 'in the general boggledybotch' of a language that has words, images and ideas flying across the page like 'alphabet bricks' after a bomb blast. Like the robot bomb-disposal expert which negotiates its way through one of these poems, verbal antennae quivering, Carson negotiates his way through the explosive minefield of Irish politics, Irish history, Irish literature and Irish lore. Words, phrases, slogans, catch cries, jargon and military and technical phraseology are dusted down, polished to a sheen and restored to the tower of poetry.

The *opus operandi* (to quote one poem's title) of these intricate sonnets, sequences and series of interlinking poems is to delve extensively into the resources of 'the deep grammar of the handshake, the shibboleths of *aitch* and *haitch*'. Invigilating the overlapping languages of the Babel that is Belfast, where even proper nouns are improper in the conflict ('Some were Paddy, and some were Billy') is Carson's highly original way of picking through the linguistic rubble that survives an explosion. This is the way the world ends in Belfast, not with a bang but with a verbal outburst.

Having the first poem in Irish with a French title is a way of announcing that, for Carson, English is merely one among many available languages and, as the title of the second poem puts it, a 'Second Language' for him, having been brought up in an Irish-speaking home. And it is in that long, autobiographical poem he introduces the 'wordy whorls and braids and skeins and spiral helices' of an English diction that is concatenated at every hand's turn into a litany of local language.

> Shipyard hymns
> Then echoed from the East: gantry-clank
>      and rivet-ranks, Six-County hexametric
> Brackets, bulkheads, girders, beams and
>      stanchions; convocated and Titanic.

(Those 'Six-County hexametric' lines which Carson has developed into a distinctive and identifiable style are not only too long to be properly quoted in these columns, but even too long to fit the margins of his publisher's pages.) That single word 'Titanic', for example, bears within the poem a multiplicity of meaning, the classical myths meeting the local legends, as that doom-laden liner, built in the Belfast shipyards, sinks into another situation. But the poem sails on through seas of memory and desire to where 'the future looms into the mouth incessantly'. And incessantly the mouth sings out its ever-changing, ever active songs.

Two precedents for this astounding poetic performance are invoked in the book – one classical, one modern. Like Eliot in *The Waste Land* ('What Tiresias *sees*, in fact, is the substance of the poem'), Carson turns to Ovid for a similar purpose – the convocation of ancient and modern worlds – but from an entirely different perspective, both politically and linguistically. Three sections of Ovid's *Metamorphoses* dealing with the violent fates of Persephone, Hecuba and Memnon are translated into the social and political argot of contemporary

Belfast: 'Powers-That-Be'; 'touts'; 'Troubles'; 'hunger strike'; 'no-go zone'; 'Prods and Taigs'; 'civil war'; 'burning each other out'. The parallels are not insisted upon. Carson is too subtle a poet to let the language do other than linger in the links between the ages. Yet the classical connotations add a significantly dramatic dimension to this account of the Ulster conflict, keeping the idiosyncrasies of Carson's approach in check.

A further precedent is more modern. Like Eliot again, Carson is drawn towards Baudelaire's verses and vision. Echoes of his celebrated *Correspondances*, translated into Carson's vibrant diction, with its synaesthesia endorsed by a further translation of Rimbaud's *Le Bateau Ivre*, offers a modern model for the 'acoustic perfume' these pages exude. That sense of correspondence, introduced in 'Second Language', where as one line in the same poem puts it, 'this one's slate-blue gaze is correspondent to another's new born eyes', is everywhere at play in these poems as the aroma of the acoustics wafts through the warp and weft of a process that is often comic in its musical timing. There is an extensive use, at times comic, of one form of poetic correspondence, rhyme. Translations may be seen as another. Translating Baudelaire's *L'Albatros*, with its ungainly image of the poet as a 'Great Auk' – 'bedraggled, ugly, awkward, how pathetic' – is a recognition that the further correspondence between the poet ('Prince of Clouds') and his people ('Jack Tars') is often comic, intractable and irrepressibly humorous.

Yet, for all the dazzle of their dactyls, the aura of their 'alexandrine tropes', the intricacy and the ingenuity of the rhymes and cross rhymes – listen, for example, to the 'tang of aromatic speech' in the delicately melodic 'On Not Remembering Some Lines of a Song' – the strength of the poems comes from being grounded in a particular place, Belfast, which becomes a vortex of 'agendas, bricks and mortar, interfaces'. The tunes that emanate from that blighted city and its environs are original, inventive and intriguing. While showing little affinity with the traditional metrical norms of English prosody, they owe less to any modernist idea of *vers libre*. The rhythmical impulse that emanates from these lines is one derived from the florid elaborations of traditional Irish music.

Listen to the first line of 'Bagpipe Music': 'He came lilting down the brae with a blackthorn stick the thick of a shotgun...' Within a line that lilt has transformed itself, metamorphosed itself if you like, into a semi-senseless indulgence in sound: *'blah dithery dump a doodle scattery idle fortunoodle...'* And

the poem danders along into an intricately tuned account of khaki-clad soldiers and balaklava-faced terrorists slipping in and out of the landscape, guns blazing, while the verbal equivalent of a bagpipe air drones away in the cluttered background. Among many other things, it offers an ironic and up-to-date riposte to the Louis MacNeice poem of the same title, even exploding its primer in one line – *'Scrake nithery lou a mackie nice wee neice ah libralassie ...'* It is, like many of the poems, an astonishing performance, one that needs to be read repeatedly to register its resonances.

It would be disingenuous to suggest anything more than an oblique correspondence between Carson and Eliot, although both share an affinity with that magisterial linguistic card-sharper, James Joyce. Their differences are more instructive. Carson is the Paganini of poetry, a virtuoso of verse playing *con brio furioso* whose every collection becomes more animated in its trills and thrills. *First Language* is *The Waste Land* written on uppers, not downers: 'We'd done a deal of blow', begins one poem called 'Grass', which then slithers along a different vocabulary to the demotic of the pub scene in 'A Game of Chess' with 'those pills I took, to bring it off'. Carson's prose work, *A Pocket Guide to Irish Traditional Music*, gestures towards a different sense of tradition to that endorsed by the author of 'Tradition and the Individual Talent'. And Carson's approach to religion and politics is far more circumspect than that of Eliot; more a case of after strange words than after strange gods. Yet, for all their divergences, both poets have honestly and intently addressed themselves to the dialect of their respective tribes. For that, and for the numerous incidental excitations of this absorbing collection, I somehow think the Old Possum would have approved this award, granted by the Poetry Book Society, in his name.

**T.S. Eliot was a founder of the Poetry Book Society and, in his honour and to celebrate its 40th anniversary last year, the Society inaugurated the T.S. Eliot Prize, worth £5,000, for the best collection of poetry published in 1993. The PBS hopes to announce this year's prize in August. Ciaron Carson's previous three collections have all received awards: the latest being the *Irish Times*/Aer Lingus Irish Literature Prize for Poetry for *Belfast Confetti* in 1991. The Poetry Book Society has recently moved, to: Book House, 45 East Hill, London SW18 2QZ; Tel: 081 870 8403.**

## MICHAEL LONGLEY

## *According to Pythagoras*

When in good time corpses go off and ooze in the heat
Creepy-crawlies breed in them.  Bury your prize bull
(A well-known experiment) – and from the putrid guts
Swarm flower-crazy bees, industrious country-types
Working hard, as did their host, with harvest in mind.
An interred war-horse produces hornets.  Remove
A shore-crab's hollow claw, lay it to rest: the result
Is a scorpion charging with its tail bent like a hook.
Worms cosy in cocoons of white thread grow into
Butterflies, souls of the dead.  Any farmer knows that.

Germs in mud generate green frogs: legless at first
They soon sprout swimming and jumping equipment.
A she-bear's cub is a lump of meat whose stumpy
Non-legs she licks into shape in her own image.
The honey-bees' larvae born in those waxy hexagons
Only get feet and wings later on.  That's obvious.
Think of peacocks. eagles, doves, the bird-family
As a whole, all starting inside eggs: hard to believe.
There's a theory that in the grave the backbone rots
Away and the spinal cord turns into a snake.

The fundamental interconnectedness of all things
Is incredible enough, but did you know that
Hyenas change sex? The female mounted by a male
Just minutes before, becomes a male herself.  Then
There's the chameleon that feeds off wind and air
And takes the colour of whatever it's standing on.
Air transforms lynxes' urine into stones and hardens
Coral, that softly swaying underwater plant.
I could go on and on with these scientific facts.
If it wasn't so late I'd tell you a whole lot more.

*Michael Longley won the Whitbread Poetry Award for* **Gorse Fires**
*(Secker & Warburg, 1991). Poems: 1963-1983 is published by Penguin.*

# Border Conflict

## by Carol Rumens

**Clair Wills,**
*Improprieties: Politics and Sexuality in
Northern Irish Poetry,*
OUP, £11.95,
ISBN 0 19 818 239 2

Why does contemporary Northern Irish poetry, in robust defiance of gloomier predictions, continue to flourish, and even blaze trails through the post-modern jungle? Clair Wills suggests some answers in her Introduction: the pressure from the Troubles on poets to breach lyric reticence, a lively argument with 'tradition and its pieties' (the literary equivalent of Revisionism), academic and American influences, etc. Interestingly, she sees the trajectory of all three poets chosen for analysis (Muldoon, McGuckian, Paulin) as moving outwards into the public arena, and not as retrenchment into a fortress of politically necessary, or at least culturally expedient, secrecy. This is usually said to be true only of Paulin. Yet there is a sense in which territorial rivalry plays a role in creating the languages of these poetries. You famously cannot throw a stone in Belfast without hitting a poet. Style is poetic territorialism (and sometimes terrorism?): the intenser the stylization, the more post-modern (though not necessarily the better) the poetry.

Wills yokes her three poets in terms of a strategy she calls Impropriety, denoting, as well as public 'expansion' of the lyric, infringements of sexual privacy, formal dispossession, and the transgression of all kinds of border. (Metaphors shift shape as fast and furiously in post-mod. criticism as in poetry!) She does not relate her Improper Trinity to the literary canon, a pity, because all have important stylistic or territorial forebears: MacNeice for Muldoon, Hewitt for McGuckian, Rodgers for Paulin – not to mention the senior contemporaries with whom they are in dialogue.

It could be argued that the current strength of Northern Irish poetry owes much to its extreme *propriety* towards the tradition, and it's worth mentioning that Wills's 'younger' poets now form a pantheon, variously pedestalled, for the truly young poets of Northern Ireland. But of course the narrow focus brings rewards in concentration on these richly metaphorical and/or referential texts.

The chapter on Medbh McGuckian stands out for several reasons. There is a reading of 'The Dream Language of Fergus' in relation to three essays by Osip Mandelstam that is especially illuminating. It reveals that, as far as any writer can be a deep source for another if approachable only via translation, it is Mandelstam, for whom words are sometimes domestic, as well as etymological, utensils ('hollow bodies' to borrow a phrase from McGuckian, infinitely fillable and steeped) who, of all the 'European' poets, is McGuckian's mentor – and not only in *On Ballycastle Beach*.

Wills convincingly challenges the conventional, sentimental view of McGuckian's work as a kind of holistic, maternal universe, showing that violence and disruption threaten even her cosiest interiors. And, by drawing on published interviews, she demonstrates how cannily this poet lays claim to public resonance by making more than one text (the poem) available to her readers. (Throw a stone in Belfast and you'll hit either a poet or an interview with Medbh McGuckian.) The full ambivalence of McGuckian regarding bafflement *v.* accessibility is revealed in her willingness to allow the meta-text to elucidate, and sometimes mischievously obfuscate, the metaphor.

All three poets interrogate that most proper of naturalized-English metrical lines, the Iambic Pentameter. Paulin's recent poetry is as much a failure (self-induced) of the art of lineation as a failure to achieve 'an alternative vision of the political'. Does Muldoon really 'deconstruct' the sonnet, or reinvigorate it? Like all post-mod. critics, Wills fights shy of aesthetic evaluation, and evades the subjectivity of assigning emotional tone-colour. In her reading of the sonnet, 'Quoof', she lists all the salient points but gives little sense of taking pleasure in the poem's self-mocking wit or the tenderness and grace of its ultimate 'turn'. (It also appears that she underplays his use of fully traditional grammatical markers, perhaps because Muldoon's syntax is Gaelic-influenced English rather than 'Standard'.) However, Wills gets strongly to grips with her material when dealing with national and historical reference. Overall, her book seems to me a valuable guide for English readers curious as to how and why poetry in Northern Ireland sustains a public resonance, despite the fact that 'Impropriety', as a concept, doesn't fully explain why such an infuriated, and infuriating, place matters so intensely to its poets, even those (two of the three featured here) who no longer live there.

## TOM PAULIN

### *On The Windfarm*

No thread to the wind
— no thread at all
it may weave clouds
may stretch their thunderheads
and their anvils
or bang like a hammer
— it can bang down really hard
like the *bora* in Trieste
that nearly broke Stendhal's arm
twice a week for a month

or it can soothe and sigh
for someone anyone
to smile and be happy
- *oh say you love her mr captain*
  *say you love mummy*
  *oh say it say it!*

but there's still no thread here
— contingent as speech
the wind's always guilty
of a total lack of backbone
and if you should seed
some prairie tornado
— drop dry ice from an airplane
that rational enterprise is doomed
the wind it veers off
to underline *storm damage*
in another corner of the state
— as well ask some spinning demon
if he carries a condom

quite so humphs the windscholar
that wind it's history
history in the making of course
and solid as action
watch out or you'll reap —

don't give me that!
the windfarmer jumps in
pragmatic as the blades
on his aluminum mill
it's a willing worker the wind

why Benjamin Franklin
he was a windfarmer too
that kite and that key
they wouldn't never've
got off of the ground
if it hadn't been for the wind

no wind no sound
no life no culture
the grass would never grow
nor the clover neither
there would be no lithographs by Paul Klee
— *no Not durch Dürre*
no Paul Klee either

so the wind
it isn't so much everything
— in that rather spent phrase
everything which is the case
as the rock on which
the true church of language
is forever building itself
then falling back down
the wind gives
the wind denies
the wind is a sermon
against itself
or the sound of Peter weeping

but it's still the wind's threadlessness
that gets on my nerves
the way it shifts and wavers
then blunders out into nowhere
— if the wind can be studied
is this feckless creature a subject?

no it isn't no
definitely not
there isn't a single form of knowledge
could ever net the wind
all we can do
is try to avoid
the heavy the hard
and the poisonous winds

those who try to confront them
are doomed to more than disappointment

for as Herodotus records
there used to be a very small nation
called the Psylli
the Psylli they declared war
on one of the worst winds there is
the desert wind the simoom
it's a dirty heavy
a highly toxic wind
and the Psylli hated it very badly
it dried away the water
in their stone tanks
it made their children ill


so the Psylli gathered spears bows and
                                    arrows
they stretched new ostrich skins on their
                                    shields
and practised slinging pebbles
– a prayer and a signal
they began their march
deep into the desert

the simoom duly came down
battle was engaged
a purple darkness hung
across the western corner
of the land called Psylli
– dark dark it was
on top of the noontide darkness
night inside night

come dawn
– a double dawn
come its fluttery suthery silence
no tracks in the sand
no Psylli
– all gone
gone every one of that tiny nation

had they only but spoken
to Franklin! cries the windfarmer
he'd have put on his mason's apron
he'd have beat that storm in the desert
he'd have beaten it hollow

---

## THE SOCIETY OF AUTHORS

invites entries for the

## 1995 ERIC GREGORY AWARDS

for the encouragement of young poets

Among previous winners have been:

Adrian Mitchell, Geoffrey Hill, Jenny Joseph, Stuart Conn, Ted Walker, John Fuller, Derek Mahon, Michael Longley, Robin Fulton, Seamus Heaney, Hugo Williams, Brian Patten, Andrew Motion, Tom Paulin, Christopher Reid, Medbh McGuckian, Robert Minhinnick, Michael Hulse, Blake Morrison, Simon Rae, Alan Jenkins, Steve Ellis, Jeremy Reed, Alison Brackenbury, Martin Stokes, Hilary Davies, Michael O'Neill, Deirdre Shanahan, Martyn Crucefix, Mick Imlah, Jamie MacKendrick, Bill Smith, Carol Ann Duffy, Iain Bamforth, Graham Mort, Adam Thorpe, Mick North, Lachlan Mackinnon, Oliver Reynolds, Peter McDonald, Maura Dooley, Stephen Knight, Michael Symmons Roberts, Gwyneth Lewis, Roddy Lumsden, Glyn Maxwell, Jill Dawson, Eleanor Brown, Joel Lane, Deryn Rees-Jones, Gerard Woodward, Nicholas Drake, Maggie Hannan, Julia Copus, Alice Oswald, Steven Blyth, Kate Clanchy, Giles Goodland,

In 1994 five awards totalling £27,000 were made.

**A candidate must be British by birth, under the age of 30, and may submit a published or unpublished collection of belles-lettres, Poetry or Drama-Poems. (Not more than 30).**
**Closing date: 31 October 1994**

Details from: Awards Secretary, THE SOCIETY OF AUTHORS, 84 Drayton Gardens, London SW10 9SB

# Dwelling with the Tongue

## by Sarah Maguire

**Tom Paulin,**
*Walking a Line,*
Faber, £5.99
ISBN 0 571 17081 1

N issen huts, bungalows, carports, studios, bars: hardly a poem goes by in Tom Paulin's glorious new collection, *Walking a Line,* without some building or other being brought to notice. And not only the building but its living space, its social and historical nexus, its *place*. This architectural sensitivity is nothing new in Paulin's poetry. From the very beginning his poems featured the 'gantries, mills and steeples', the 'miles of terrace-houses' and the 'strange museums' of Adam houses and Georgian rectories in which 'History could happen' (in the title poem of *The Strange Museum*). This is not a history of external events or rote-learned dates, but a rich, complex history in which both subjectivity, and objects themselves, find their meanings in relation to one another: 'Caught in the nets of class,/ History became carpets, chairs', he writes in his anti-Hegelian poem, 'The Idea in History'. Paulin is not so much a poet of cities, of the seething interrelationships and juxtapositions of buildings, detritus and humans, but of the building out on a limb, of 'The Bungalow on the Unapproved Road' in *Fivemiletown*. Even the bedsits that populate the first two books have 'The dull ripe smell of gas' ('Second-Rate Republics') of the deracinated suburbs, are lonely in their proximity. And what is notable about the buildings and dwellings (Paulin is still grappling with Heidegger) in *Walking a Line* is their hesitancy, their provisionality, what, in 'A History of the Tin Tent', Paulin calls their 'throwaway permanence': 'sheets of corrugated iron/beaverjoints purlins joists/ wire nails and matchboard lining/ were packed into kits/ so complete societies/ could be knocked and bent/ into sudden being'. 'Europe became a desert', he reminds us, 'so these tents could happen'. But now 'they're almost like texts/ no one wants to read/ – texts prefabs caves/ a whole aesthetic in reverse'. It is from his exemplary readings of such homeless constructions that Paulin gathers the materials with which to build his own texts.

The blurb of the book tells us that its title 'is taken from a statement by Paul Klee ... [who] presides over its contents as a sort of guardian angel'. We meet Klee in the book's first poem, 'Klee/Clover', improvising, cutting 'squares of canvas/ from the wings and fuselage' of biplanes that crashed onto the airfield where he was drafted during the First World War. Like Paulin, Klee makes art from the provisional, so that the pilots 'never knew they were flying/ primed blank canvases/ into his beautiful airfield'. Klee's delicacy, his wonderful combination of wit and seriousness, infuse this book with a grace and deftness of touch which make this Paulin's most successful and important collection to date.

Paulin's pure lyricism, combined with his acute historical and political sense in his first two books, meant far more to me than anything else written during the late 'seventies and early 'eighties, and I've continued to admire his work ever since, particularly 'The Book of Juniper' in *Liberty Tree*, which remains one of the strongest poems he's written. But there were times in that book, and in *Fivemiletown*, when I just wished he'd stop banging on, when I'd come to the end of a poem and feel somehow got at (which, I admit, is a great improvement on the feeling of complacent cleverness induced by some of his contemporaries). It was as though the sour accents of patriarchal Presbyterianism he so strenuously criticized had infected his own tongue a little too pungently. Sometimes I felt excluded from those books, in the way that I felt excluded from Paulin's pathetically narrow version of politics which informed *The Faber Book of Political Verse*. But in *Walking a Line* the righteous anger of his earlier work has mutated into something far more self-questioning. And linguistically, there's been a corresponding shift of registers. Paulin's language is still as inventive as ever, but he's abandoned the sometimes hermetic and rebarbative clumped glottals of the last two books for a more open lyricism that can be as precise as it is tender:

*sparrowgrass* is its own concept

light and wavy like the smoky bush
that grows and grows
into a soft flumy
a feathery delicacy

('Sparrowgrass')

*Walking a Line* is a delight. And one of its great delights is its critique of masculinity, as brave as anything I've seen attempted by a male poet before. There's always been a lot of jism in Paulin's books and, whilst I'm prepared to accept that this cocksure display may have been intended as a radical deconstruction through explicit exposure of the root of phallocentrism (sorry), it did all get rather tiresome after a while. Here though, the representations of gender are troubled by a 'phallic guilt'. In 'Circumstantial' Paulin's attempt to make 'poetry [from] little things/ – say bits of scrim / that plosive lid' of 'The hymen on the coffee jar/ its gilt or silver foil' leads to a feeling of unease: 'maybe also there's a small/ phallic guilt/ something niggly and annoying/ that he'll never fathom?' Time after time the poet is stymied by the problem of making metaphors appropriate to femininity, particularly to the 'fleshy oxymoron' ('Cadmus and the Dragon') of the female genitalia. How is the male poet, sensitive to feminism, to write of his desire? How can heterosexual penetration be anything other than a violation? Or worse, what if it's simply a redundant activity?

'A Taste of Blood' deals with that despair. It begins, 'At long last he believes/ that he's found a metaphor/ to explain the way it always pans out/ between the pair of them/... it begins with the hinged shell/ of an oyster'. But that means 'he can only be a claspknife/... no wonder then/ that even in the act of love/ the oyster won't open/ and allow him to enter/ all the deliciousness inside'.

A way out of this metaphorical appropriation is suggested by Klee's methodology of improvisation, of humility in the face of one's materials. Language, Paulin realises, is radically uncertain and unstable. In 'On the Windfarm' the wind is 'the rock on which/ the true church of language/ is forever building itself/ then falling back down'. (Interestingly enough, in 'Cadmus and the Dragon' 'the bottomless vagina' is seen as 'easy effortless as a windsock/ infinite as language'.) In 'The New

Year' Paulin confronts the historical and political deceptions of language. What troubles him here is 'my one language' in which 'every sentence/ builds itself/ on risk/ and an ignorance/ of what's been hacked down/ or packed up'.

It is this ignorance which the protagonist of 'A Taste of Blood' fails to appreciate. In his masculine desire to name and control his lover, he fails to acknowledge both the history of such an appropriation (the whole edifice of 'love' poetry is built on this naming) or to comprehend the possibility of female agency. This is yet another heterosexual encounter devoid of mutuality. But in the delightful celebration of cunnilingus, 'L', pleasure moves from the guilty phallus to the hesitant explorations of the tongue.

Here, instead of attempting to find the appropriate metaphor for female genitalia, language is allowed to open out the poem into a shifting set of metaphors which invoke the erotic pleasures of the tongue, abandoning attempts to fix or control these sensual associations: 'like a heifer drawn to the rocks/ it loves to lick salt/ and dwell on the sea's minerals'. In naming and questioning his own pleasures, in pausing to reflect (as Klee did) on the significance of the small detail, taking it for a walk into its own context, its own history, Paulin has found a flexible and generous poetic method which is both tender and daring. '[T]his tongue thing's a supple instrument', 'L' concludes,

kinda decent and hardworking
and often more welcome than the penis
– too many poems speak of that member
maybe it's time I unbuttoned my tongue?

## PAULA BURNETT
### *Late September*

Driving out new shivers in a steaming bath,
my summer skin sloughs off. The radio barks
at racism cornered in the Isle of Dogs.

'Sea-dogs are supposed to know, aren't they, about need
for harbour? docks are supposed to breed
bright browns, not apart-hate.'

The nation contemplates its navel. We reach
out our brown arms across the water
but our bellies stay stubbornly white.

## Water Works

### by John Lucas

**Peter Redgrove,**
*The Cyclopean Mistress:*
*Selected Short Fiction,*
Bloodaxe, £7.95,
ISBN 1 85224 207 8
*My Father's Trapdoors,*
Cape, £7.00,
ISBN 0 224 03896 6
*The Laborators,*
Taxus Press, £6.50,
ISBN 1 873012 47 0
**Neil Roberts,**
*The Lover, The Dreamer and The World:*
*The Poetry of Peter Redgrove,*
Sheffield Academic Press, £19.50 hbk,
ISBN 1 8507 5416 0
£11.95 pbk  ISBN 1 8507 5714 3

'**A**n epic from Bob Southey every spring,' Byron sardonically remarked. Peter Redgrove may not be quite that productive but he certainly seems to be an unstoppable force, These three new books – one prose, two poetry – join a list of publications that is now within sight of its half-century. I'm not sure, though, that they will be among the most memorable. At all events, *The Cyclopean Mistress* is a bit of a yawn. Fiction, like responsibility, may begin in dreams, but it shouldn't end there. Too many of the pieces in this collection are offered as transcriptions of dreams, his own or those of a woman. Others aspire to the dream-like, with all that means in the way of woozy writing. 'There is a young deer crowned with a wreath of mist standing stock-still at the coppice-edge. It turns and merges with the trees, suddenly invisible, like a soul of the trees. It is a deer that stands like a portal ...' ('Moon Rising Over Richmond Park'). Or – 'This is a dream she had on the second day of her menstrual bleeding. She was trampling the grapes in a wooden vat with her partner. He held in his hand a sample secret of his strength, the vine, with its great bunches of grapes. That same strength was being trampled underfoot' ('Second Day'). As Eric Morecambe might have said, 'There's no answer to that'. Or

this: 'Then I was living in a shop-front. Everybody could see all my details as they passed' ('Greedy Green'). Or this: 'The entering of her was like eating a little spoonful of golden syrup warmed over a candle-flame. Her cunt gave off a round heat that was itself a dream. There was instant hypnosis, and an immense river-bridge between us that was slowly and inexorably vibrating' ('A Crystal of Industrial Time'). I don't know, though: 'immense river-bridge'. I mean, I realise some men boast about the length of their pricks, but this is ridiculous.

It's a fault that can invade the poems. In the often fine title poem of the Cape volume Regrove can't resist saying of his 'wedding-tackle' that he doesn't want to use it as a wand to 'disappear' his woman, since 'I an rather too fond of disappearing it myself,/But I also use it to empower us both'. Oh, that's alright, then. You could of course say that such writing comes of Redgrove's refusal to be ironically aware, that it's the price to be paid for his commitment to what, for want of a better phrase, I will call his belief in the sacredly profane. 'Ovulating on St Valentine's Day,/ She is odorous and voluptuous after her bath' one of the poems in *The Laborators* begins. Yet some, including this one, seem all-too self-conscious; and in that case – or in *any* case – haven't we the right to expect a cancelling of dead language ('There was a diamond blazing at the cleavage'), of the olde-worldy ('I saw plain what they meant'), of slack phrasing (men jealous 'to become premenstrual or pregnant' are said to sing 'Not like light-carving jewels or throaty birds/But in squeaky voices like tightly-blown balloons/Tested with a thumb')? Too much attention to the message, too little to the medium. A like fault cumbers Neil Roberts' sympathetic, not to say rapturous, account of Redgrove's work. Roberts is excellent at teasing out the often difficult meanings of the poetry and prose, but good and bad get bundled together as though there were no differerence between them.

My examples of less than satisfactory writing are chosen at random and could be multiplied. There is also a problem, it seems to me, with the narrative procedure of many of the poems: where they start, where they end. In fact, they don't so much end as stop – as dreams, of course do. It may be that Redgrove is instinctively (or knowingly?) aligning himself with Paul Valéry's contention that verse 'wanders around circuitously, winding back on itself, repeating similar gestures ... and is not directed towards any single definite end'. Its energies are not those of prose, protestant, masculine, with its teleological determination to 'march as straight as possible' towards an end always in view. Redgrove's poems don't end with that satisfying click of a box shutting which Yeats thought – or at least said – told him a poem was finished. On the other hand, one of the best poems in *My Father's Trapdoors*, 'Stained Waterworks' is a lovely, wittily attentive account of the six stages by which 'riverwater gross as gravy' emerges clean from taps. The antiphonal cadences of Christopher Smart's *Jubilate Agno* are threaded into Redgrove's lines: 'For it is a hall of twenty pyramids upside down.... // For, these twenty pyramids are decanters/And there are strong lights at their points'; but this is part of the poem's relishing of the waterworks' mundane alchemical process. And Redgrove can throw off a small lyric like 'Lamps and Fire' with the accomplished ease of a master. There are half-a-dozen such poems scattered among these two collections, but two into one would have gone nicely.

## JULIA COPUS

## *The Art of Interpretation*

A plain wood table, the obligatory
vase of flowers, the writer's head bent low
over his work.  At the far end, a window.

Open.  Apart from this there is little
to help us with the story: the room is left
deliberately bare, inviting us

To speculate.  Consider, for instance,
the window as eye.  Is it looking out
or looking in? Notice, too, the dark, plum

Sheen of the nib; and the pen, not poised
but resting, heavy, on the page.  Unused.
Do you see how the artist plays the light

Off against the shade? The candle, also,
is misleading: I advise you to ignore
the warmth of its glow.  Drop the temperature

A little.  Allow your eyes to wander
over the shadows, where the details are:
the clearly-labelled Absinthe flask, half full,

Half empty; the sweeping lines of the words
in the open letter, just visible
under the lifeless curl of his fingers.

Now turn up the volume of background noise,
the pub's detritus in the street outside.
Bring it level with the window.  Then cut.

## Airy Shapes
### by Philip Gross

**Vicki Feaver,**
*The Handless Maiden,*
Cape, £6.00
ISBN 0 224 03892 3

**N**o-one planning a poetry career would do it like this: a first collection published in 1981, then, thirteen years on, a little flush of competition winners and this second book. It arrives just on cue to show up the pettiness of marketing poetry by 'generations'. Are these poems 'new' or 'old'? The voice in them is fresh and fierce:

I'd have commandeered a crane
if I could, got the welders at Jarrow
to heat me an iron the size of a tug
to flatten the house.

But there is a lot of living in it. The poems refer to long relationships and personal changes, a life that has passed through stages, sweet and sour. The effect is not one of hindsight – passion is not spent but clarified, like her mother's crab apple jelly (also long in the making) in the poem of that name: 'as clear and shining/ as stained glass and the colour of fire'.

The fire is anger. Yes, there is sex, too, most often as a 'fox stink', 'the bitch in me', 'sticky, stained sheets'. If there is pleasure in it, that pleasure is very close to rage. From Judith hacking Holofernes' head off ('easy/ like slicing through fish') to the mild dinner-party hostess who appears in the doorway with a fistful of knives ('carvers/ bunched in her hands/ like dangerous flowers') the book is full of women who might just, at last, suddenly, wreak vengeance. As the opening poem, 'Marigolds', nailed its colours to the mast: 'we are killers, can tear the heads/ off men's shoulders' – I braced myself for a blast of collective anger, the voice not of a woman but of Women with a capital W. By page three I was unbracing. Her 'Circe' who starts as one of a canon of female myth-figures ready to be reclaimed for female power and wildness suddenly leaps into precise and individual detail, having her way with Ulysses 'in the damp, ripe, gooseberry rot/ of my sheets'.

In the end, it was me who sent him away.
It made me too sad: hearing
my name on his tongue
like the hiss of a tide withdrawing.

Several male artists – Lucien Freud, Andrew Wyeth, Roger Hilton – are taken coolly and accurately to task for their use of women models. The first is seen serving 'something – still loose/ in the world – that likes nothing better/ than to be fed on a naked girl/ with two fried eggs'. (A subtler moment than a short quote indicates – the protest blends not only with humour, but an earlier image of the woman's own foot on crushed eggs in a curlew's nest.) The poem on Hilton's 'Oi Yoi Yoi' is quite genial:

As a woman I ought to object.
But she looks happy enough.
And which of us doesn't occasionally
want one of the old gods to come down
and chase us over the sands?

A concession, clearly, from strength, not weakness.

Woven in among the myths and paintings, there are overtly personal poems, which sketch what might be a biography, from childhood in 'Dawlish 1947' through puberty to marriage, family life, disaffection and conflict. The mood ranges from ironic irritation ('you have that faraway look/ as if it's all going on/ in another room/ on another floor/ of another century') to the near-murderous. But it is the direct address of these poems, where the 'I' is individual and close to home, that wins my complete acquiescence to the myths re-entered later in the book. 'Judith' and 'Esther' speak with grief, rage and loathing; both would be powerful poems out of any context ('Judith' won a Forward individual poem prize) but seeing them placed in a whole collection gives them an authority that goes beyond any partisan (male? female? sexist? feminist?) response.

Paradoxically, it is the most domestic subject in the book that most convinces me. 'Ironing' charges the most ordinary of household jobs with passion – 'my iron flying over sheets and towels/ like a sledge chased by wolves over snow,/ the flex, twisting and crinking/ until the sheath frayed ...' Then there are the 'years I ironed nothing./ I put the iron in a high cupboard./ I converted to crumpledness'. Then a return, which suddenly looks like the writer's return to poetry, concentrating that old energy into something fine but intensely physical: 'an airy shape with room to push/ my arms, breasts, lungs, heart into'. A good description of these poems. Welcome back.

## From Berlin to the Emerald City

### by Ian McMillan

**John Hartley Williams,**
*Double,*
Bloodaxe, £6.95,
ISBN I 85224 273 6
**Peter Didsbury,**
*That Old Time Religion,*
Bloodaxe, £6.95,
ISBN I 85224 255 8

I was going to start off this review with a bit of musing about the idea of a 'mainstream' in British Poetry, and how these two mavericks are well outside it, rowing their own rickety boats down an unfashionable trickle. The trouble is, it's simply not true, and in a post-*New Poetry* world these two are as much a part of the mainstream as anybody else, and the mainstream is a more diverse thing for it.

John Hartley Williams breaks as many rules as he can, often by just being alive. He doesn't live in England, for a start: he lives and teaches in Berlin, and his poems mix a European overview (or helicopter view, as I heard a teacher describe it the other day) with a laconic, almost American diction. The result is, thank God, very unEnglish: 'And that lustreless boulder, my car,/Rotted its immobility downward,/ Down thru the tarmac and the clay'. The movement in the poem reflects the movement of the car, and 'lustreless boulder' is, in context, perfect. There are poems here about the Berlin Wall: 'There was a solitary rabbit, & a man with a shoot to kill policy,/ and far off, a jeep without lights' – and life in Berlin: 'Next to the dogs, which ran hither and thither on wires,/ lay the sky, where it had fallen down/ & nobody thought to pick it up, nail it back,/ but all walked round it' – as well as poems about London: 'We drive back over Hangar Lane./ Silent cows are standing in the fields,/ Their breath clouding the air./ They remind me of/ Accessories for disabled drivers,/ Keeping their brown eyes thoughtfully on nothing'.

It seems to me that Williams's great skill (like those other Williams's, C.K. and W.C.) is to make the places and people he's writing about seem to be absolutely central to the concerns of poetry, now and always. Sounds simple, sounds obvious, but think how many times you hold a poem up to the light and none comes through; think how many poems about lovers that turn out to be cats, or visits to dying relatives, or touristy impressions of France, simply don't stand up to the weight of all the poems that have been written before. Williams's poems do; they are vitally important poems, and at the same time vitally authentic poems. Of course he's living in a vital place at a vital time, and perhaps it would be harder to write from the point of view of an apprentice-weaver in Cleckheaton in 1848, and make the poems universal, but I think Williams could do it, given his view of the bleakness and arbitrariness of history:

So I bought a ticket for the museum
and went round the dismal rooms
and felt happy there was no fire burning
in the great hall at the centre of the maze.

### Peter Didsbury

Peter Didsbury, on the other hand, breaks as many rules as he can – often by just being alive. He's an archæologist for Humberside County Council rather than being a teacher or a writer-in-residence, and although he lives in Hull his poems owe more to the Emerald City in Oz than they do to Terry Street. Didsbury does what the best, rarest Science Fiction writers do: he makes you believe the unbelievable things he's telling you. You could call it suspension of disbelief except for that phrase's assumption that sooner or later the disbelief will come back, like malaria; with Didsbury you believe for ever, because he creates a world that seems so right: 'What luck!/ There's a long-case clock in a meadow of wind and herbs/ with its face turned towards him,/ and it's not as late as he thought'. Other poets might expand on the long-case clock in the meadow, weaving whole lines and stanzas around it, but Didsbury has enough confidence to leave it alone once the explorer 'observes it long enough to make sure/ that the minute hand is moving'. Searchers for meaning behind the poems will be disappointed or frustrated; as readers we can be much happier with Didsbury's work if we just accept it as a factual report about the way things are, and then we can just settle back and enjoy the music of what happens (to steal a phrase): 'I'm drinking tea in a furniture store,/ idly thinking of Phoebus, the sun-god,/

when a sky-blue sofa on which a youth reclines/ glides slowly through the cafeteria,/ pushed by a couple of girls in nylon shop-coats' ('Staff Only'). At his best Didsbury creates heartbreakingly moving and original lines that make me gasp, particularly in his shorter poems –

I loved the rain, but always suffered badly from post-pluvial tristesse.

My best wet afternoon was in the mouth of a disused railway tunnel, behind me the mile-long carbon-encrusted

dark

('The Shorter "Life"'),

– which seems to find an echo in the beautiful second stanza of 'Common Property': 'I revealed in turn how obsessed I'd become/ with the notion of raindrops falling inside the chimney,/ adding to thousands of feet through clandestine air/ another thirty through the centre of my house'.

On the larger canvas, and there are a number of longer poems here, Didsbury doesn't work quite so well for me; I'm not entirely sure why, but the long form seens to dilute the lad's strengths a little, although there are still examples of lines you wish you could buy in the shops: 'And as if, held in a nimbus of black sand,/ the glassy basalt pillbox of the island,/ were nodding like a head from the eighteenth century'.

Williams and Didsbury are both originals, writing like nobody else I can think of (and I read a lot of poems) and their originality lies, I think, in their confidence with language. There aren't really any new ideas here (are there anywhere?) but does it matter when the ideas we've heard before are presented in such stunning ways: 'Trying to find the Way Out,/ One room led to another, wrongly./ A hippo was receiving bellywash,/ adjusting the vertical hold on its yawn./ A sign upon the wall read:/ Last one to leave can keep the door' (Williams, 'The Zoo'); 'Way it gets dark here./ Down by the water/ the sky turns out its pockets/ and goes to sleep on the grass' (Didsbury: 'One Mile Wide').

What will be very interesting will be to see how these two poets develop over the next few years. It's not as though we're welcoming New Generationers here: Didsbury is 48 and this is his third full length collection; Williams is 52 and this is his fourth book. Their voices have been formed, their techniques have been honed, and I think that in the next decade, barring accidents, they'll both be producing work that'll put them head and shoulders over most of their contemporaries. It's only a hunch, but if I'm right, remember where you read it first; if I'm wrong, I'll make out that Frederick Raphael said it in *PN Review*.

## JOHN HARTLEY WILLIAMS
## *Jungle Drums*

No Lana Turner in tight-waisted khaki
To hand him the rifle to plug the wall-eyed buffalo
A wet slap is the map springing back in his face
Stewart Granger will not rescue him now

Then he stumbles on a damp hill
Sweet luggage of memory! It brings back
Melancholy mothers of the moon
Girls who talked endlessly in tents
Porters who played rag time on the portable piano
And the final commeuppance of Dr Abuze
The toppled evil Emperor of Baboof, leaving him
Free to mount the Throne of Potties, alone

How he orders the stained suitcase of her body opened
With trembling fingers, unpacks the cool, still-covered bones!

## MAUREEN WILKINSON
### *The Virtual Reality Shop*

*'Sometimes I think we have uncovered a new planet, but one we're inventing
instead of discovering.' Jaron Lanier:* **Cyberspace***.*

She lived within the dark shoal of the forest,
where the trees were half fish; their clenched oblations of earth
anchoring her.  So gladly and vehemently
did those wooden whales spout their sap to the sky,
that the clouds were unable to land, and countless birds
rode high in that green turbulence.

Sometimes she embraced the trees in her naked arms,
pressing her face to the bark, to feel through her skin
the subtle vibration of flutes.  Her footsteps netted
the forest in constellations.  She named each day
after herself; and the trees were her vaulting boys,
and her dancing beaux, and her solemn husbands, counting
*'days upon days upon days'* in their coinage of leaves.

Night-times she straddled high branches, riding to nowhere,
though her dreams flew like horses;

and when the trees fell, then she sawed them up into slices,
divining the circles which spread from a central moment.
She spat on two fingers to mark out a spittle o'clock,

before using a knife to whittle away air's white spaces,
for each tree held a replica world.  Everything was her totem.

Then she carved her as she-fox, accommodating as shadow,
but always revealed by the blaze of its hair;
her as rooks, weaving crosswords, her snake-word of birdsong, her
as granite, with its single thought, which she wasn't revealing.

She fashioned the overlay labyrinths, each interlinked
like the flower of a compass.

Her carvings were pieces of miracle water,
darting with light, and the contoured grains slipping
in folds, as if wood were a clothing, grown
from the inside, and finally fitting.

She set up her shop by the road, at the edge of the woodland.
Her customers paid what they had to:

and when she grew rich she bought herself thousands of mirrors,
and built them into a maze, enclosing the forest,
and each silver cell contained trees, and a woman stepping
between them:
and when the trees fell she undid them, and each whittled woman
could unpeel to reveal a forest of women inside her.

Now her shoal of reality swims through a milky sky.
She names everything after herself,
for she rightly insists that
the world contains nothing but women,
and trees.

*Illustration by Mei Li, Central St Martin's School of Art*

# Elevenses

## by Roger Garfitt

**Patricia Beer,**
*Friend of Heraclitus,*
Carcanet, £6.95,
ISBN 1 85754 026 3

**William Şcammell,**
*Five Easy Pieces,*
Sinclair-Stevenson, £7.99,
ISBN 1 85619 315 2

**John Gohorry,**
*Talk into the Late Evening,*
Peterloo, £6.95,
ISBN 1 871471 26 5

**Clive Wilmer,**
*Of Earthly Paradise,*
Carcanet, £6.95,
ISBN 0 85635 978 5

**Gillian Clarke,**
*The King of Britain's Daughter,*
Carcanet, £6.95,
ISBN 1 85754 031 X

**Penelope Shuttle,**
*Taxing the Rain,*
OUP, £6.99,
ISBN 0 19 282993 9

**Harry Mathews,**
*A Mid-Season Sky,*
Carcanet, £8.95,
ISBN 0 85635 913 0

**John Mole,**
*Depending on the Light,*
Peterloo, £6.95,
ISBN 1 871471 38 9

**Paul Mills,**
*Half Moon Bay,*
Carcanet, £6.95,
ISBN 1 85754 000 X

**Chris Wallace-Crabbe,**
*Rungs of Time,*
OUP, £6.99,
ISBN 0 19 283160 7

**Graham Mort,**
*Snow from the North,*
Dangaroo Press, £7.95, ISBN 1 871049 92 X

Patricia Beer's *Collected Poems* (1988) established her, in the words of John Bayley, as 'one of the best poets writing in England today'. Her new collection, *Friend of Heraclitus*, is exemplary in that it consists almost entirely of necessary poems. Arising naturally out of her life in Devon, they form an informal calendar, charting the arrival of the ram in June, or a summer visit from 'our children' and 'their children', small occasions to which she manages to give an unusual resonance. The ram 'has no war in him,/ No resolution of the heroic sort,/ Yet waits up there in the dark, his harness on,/ Looking for day, as if at Agincourt', while the grandparents, lifted for a moment out of lives where they 'are old/ And sleep late after bad nights', see their family off at five o'clock on an August morning:

> We breathe cautiously in the untried air,
> Talk warily at the centre of six fields,
>
> And then comes cockcrow, swaggering up
> Out of the valley. The invisible bird
> Plumes himself. He was the one chosen
> To nail good terrified Peter. He conquers
> The dark with flying colours.

Her work derives its depth and authority from traditional sources: historical and biblical references, metre and rhyme. Yet she can be effortlessly contemporary, as in this childhood memory of a cloud crossing the beach where a friend had drowned the week before: 'As it came nearer I curled up like prey./ At my right temple it narrowed and streamed in,/ The comic strip of a ghost'. I admire her flexibility and economy, the unobtrusive rightness of her means: free verse for that childhood memory, three *a* rhymes in a quatrain to convey writer's block:

> I must start writing. That is what I do.
> Time does not give me what I want it to.
> The farm moves forward. Food goes through
> its gut.
> And I am as immobile as the view.

The language never draws attention to itself. Felicitous phrases abound but always to the point: 'the consternation of her bloodstream' in 'Footbinding', 'The rats had tired, the streets were out of breath' on 'The Night Marlowe Died'. She has something of Larkin's self-effacing gift, the ability to write verse so alive with detail that the last thing we notice is its formal control.

It's a pity that she also felt obliged to come up with a formal 'Wessex Calendar', twelve sonnets about places of literary and historical interest. Not even her sardonic wit can quite subvert English Heritage. The sequence is saved by the power of the last two sonnets, which read as if they, too, were necessary poems.

**William Scammell**'s *Five Easy Pieces* opens with a *soupçon* of self-importance: a prose memoir of his childhood, in pale imitation of Craig Raine's 'A Silver Plate'. He proceeds on first-name terms with everybody: 'Get on with you, Gavin!' (Who actually says 'Get on with you' nowadays?); 'Dear Seamus: yes ...'; 'No, Randall, no ...'; even giving Mallarmé a nudge and a wink: 'It's murder, Stéphane, ain't it? And it's fun/ dancing the metaphors'. There is a danger, once you settle yourself into the clubhouse, of turning into a bore.

And yet Scammell has forged an effective style, able to register the 'bin-liner mess/ of comfortlessness' and still rise to a purposeful eloquence, as in his celebration of 'Fruit':

> a sea and a wood joined in holy matrimony,
> wave
> and particle theory reconciled, the relish of
> exploration
> and the truly biblical joy of arriving back
> home.

The celebratory note, struck against the grain of the times, recurs throughout the book and is its surest achievement.

It is the focus that is partial. His lament for Randall Jarrell may be deeply felt, his memo to Philip Roth sharp and more than justified, but talk between literary confrères is no substitute for a real engagement. Scammell tries to make it so, dedicating a lengthy digest of Kuznetsov's *Prison Diaries* to 'all who oppose tyranny' and extending 'a frustrate, proxy, western, clean/ and useless handshake' to the students of Tiananmen Square. Several adjectives too many there. He is reaching for a rhyme with 'screen' or he might have asked himself how clean his handshake really is. 'Scandalous lies' are told in this country too. Apart from one swift glance at brutality 'roaming the state/ with a caring logo on its bib', he nowhere confronts them. Hence, perhaps, the purblindness of his 'Extempore Letter' to Seamus Heaney, an ill-judged rebuke to a man who has maintained a difficult position with delicacy and honour, and at some personal risk.

In the end, Scammell is only too pleased to be his own 'intellectual' who 'has a thousand reasons / why the case is complex', who 'struts the road,/ starts and stops a story, falls in love/ with half a dozen girls'. He satirises but indulges him, bringing him, 'like Byron ... kicking his way home through the Grand Canal'. It amounts, in the words of a line Scammell himself quotes from Bob Dylan, to 'a luxury of derision generating self-regard'.

**John Gohorry** needs to ask himself who his readers are. 'Hobbes' Whale' has a schoolboy translating Greek into Latin. The remnants of my classical education just about enable me to follow. They also authorize me to say that it really wasn't worth all the trouble. Gohorry could have achieved his effect much more simply. A pity, because the image of the aged Hobbes passing through 'a boisterous coterie of wits, fops and cullies' is one of the strongest in the book –

> He immerses his age in their repartees
> as behemoth sinks his bulk into water, eyes
> periscopes over
> the flood, and his nostrils two heaving shafts
> at waterlevel.
>
> Their wit is celerity of imagining, but unstable,
> quicksilver.
> His is steady as ever, thoughts lumbering
> towards a certainty.
> *Truth is the right ordering of names in our*
> *affirmations;*
> *he taketh it in with his eyes: his nose pierceth*
> *through snares.*

– one of them being Gohorry's overwriting. Hobbes could not simply be born: he had to become 'this crying text which even as daylight breaks/ nudges himself towards print'.

*Talk into the Late Evening* is a collection about language that threatens to sink under it. But it does contain one *tour de force*, 'An Incident in the Plaza del Zocodover, Toledo, 1584', a brilliant reconstruction of an intricately ordered society through which dark forces suddenly surface, and two taut miniatures, 'At Middle Aston' and 'On the Edge', where Gohorry has disciplined and concentrated his effects.

He also succeeds, in poems like 'Unidentified Aliens, New Mexico, 1947' and 'Under Mount Fuji', in distilling a contemporary language out of sci-fi and computer terminology. How one longs for some such possibility in the work of **Clive Wilmer**! Even in poems of personal difficulty, he seems to be writing at a scholarly remove:

> I keep two journals. In the first one there's
> A record of dreams, fantasies and fears ...

On odd days in the second – now more odd,
Alas, than ordinary – I brood on God
[...]

Sadly I can't conflate them in one text.
There I am crazed, erratic, oversexed,
Here pure, serene and earnest in my quest;
An angel here, there a tormented beast!

This is like reading the confessions of a Victorian clergyman. The poem ends with a quaint, pre-Freudian longing for 'the single mind where single truths reside', a longing reflected in the very neatness of the couplets. It's as if the formal procedure he is using invites him to divide and simplify.

There are two much better poems, 'The Garden' and 'Oasis', where the couplings are at least paradoxical:

And it is paradise I think of too
When your cool body's fluency and grace
Come near, and nearer, in this desert place
As if the Lord were beckoning through you –
  Though God is darkest when his creatures
                                             bless
And paradise is of the wilderness.

The voice of Geoffrey Hill seems to echo in the background of that poem, just as couplets derived from Dick Davis frame 'The Temple of Aphrodite'. Even the free verse in *Of Earthly Paradise* seems familiar in its procedures. All of which confirms one's impression of an imitative and highly self-conscious book in which the desire to make poetry from experience preempts the experience itself. In 'St Francis Preaching to the Birds' Wilmer argues that the birds, 'living beyond reach,/ Indifferent to meaning,/ Are made anew in speech'. When things are really made anew in speech, they do not have that slightly old-fashioned ring.

*Of Earthly Paradise* ends with a cantata, 'Caedmon of Whitby', in which Wilmer bases his recitative on a sixteenth-century translation of Bede – rather what one would expect from someone who translates St Francis' 'Canticle of the Sun' into a pastiche of the old Prayer Book. **Gillian Clarke** creates a much more interesting texture for her oratorio, *The King of Britain's Daughter*, by setting the legend of Brân and Branwen against memories of the family farm in Wales, where a rocking stone on the cliff was said to be one of Brân's slingstones. The oratorio becomes a double lament, for Branwen in exile and for her own lost childhood summers, and the language modulates from a lyric for her father's old hat –

When she gave it away [...]

she gave away mornings of forage,
beachcombings, blackberries, pebbles, eggs,
field-mushrooms with pleated linings,

his fist working it to a form
for the leveret that quivered under my hand
before it died.

– to the high style of Brân: *'taking the west wind to my heart like grief'*.

There are moments in the rest of the collection when one could wish for a greater modulation in the language. Lines like 'the sea's slippery pages/ turning forever/ at the edge of the mind' seem too easy a recourse to traditional lyric effects. Not that other notes are not struck, and struck tellingly, from the humour of 'Chip-Hog' or 'Stealing Peas' – '÷You're prettier. She's funnier." / I wished I hadn't asked' – to Clarke's satiric glimpse of a low-flying jet pilot: 'boy scaring boy off the face of his own land,/ all do and dare, and look at me, no hands', or her wry comment on 'A Photograph from Space':

North America, Europe,
drawn in light,

while Africa is a dark house,
India missing from the photograph,
relatives no one remembered to call
for the family picture.

But there is a limit to what some formal procedures can do, witness her slightly forlorn 'Lament': 'For the burnt earth and the sun put out,/ the scalded ocean and the blazing well./ For vengeance, and the ashes of language'.

The title poem of **Penelope Shuttle**'s new collection, *Taxing the Rain*, is one of several that give it a new, polemical edge. The celebration of erotic energies that was so vivid a feature of her last collection, *Adventures with My Horse*, continues in 'Trick Horse', a beautifully written description of the horse made of entwined balancing lovers in Indian erotic art, and in poems like 'Honeymoon'. 'Nuptial Arts', 'Big Cat', and 'Jesus':

and the women get drunk on the Jesus-water,
each woman sighs and aches and is blessed
                                             on her bed,
she is floating on the beloved waters,
she desires to be wet, drenched, flooded,
as she comes, she gasps, 'Sweet Jesus!'

But they seem to be tied in quite deliberately to the

title poem where rain, 'the weakest and strongest of us all', is made to pay for its privileges:

> Let rain be taxed, they say,
> for riding on our rivers
> and drenching our sleeves;
>
> for loitering in our lakes
> and reservoirs. Make rain pay its way.

It's as if the powers of renewal, which had always seemed so unfailing and unfathomable, may themselves be close to exhaustion, as if we are already reaching the point Shuttle describes in a poem that takes its title from Neruda, 'No pudieron seguir soñando':

> Whenever an earthquake occurs,
> our planet rings like a bell;
> but it has stopped dreaming.
> Not one Stone in the World is dreaming.
> The last word of all
> is in your mouth;
> slide it between my lips;
> let me taste the last of salt.

The mother-child relationship is as erotically charged in Shuttle's poetry as the man-woman relationship and that continues in a poem like 'Mademoiselle':

> She is the long and short of it,
> she is the blueness of the beetle's
> belly, she is the ivory
> fish, the clean-washed japanese
> clothes. She is
> the use of rainy weather,
> the only valuable thing ...

Now the maternal energies, too, are rising up in protest. 'Breasts' imagines both her breasts bursting out of her blouse during the ten o'clock news and landing 'thwack! against the dusty tv screen', only to be cheated of 'their many-mouth-filling vocation': 'Wasted children still gaze through burning air./ Remote and hunched, their dry mothers stare./ Drought wind toys with their brightly-beaded hair'. Penelope Shuttle has always been a skilled manipulator of language, adept at varying its textures and creating surprise, and this seems a new and timely use of her gift.

*A Mid-Season Sky* brings together **Harry Mathews'** *Poems 1954–1991*. Carcanet have published four of his novels but this is the first time his poetry has appeared in Britain. He divides his time between New York and Paris and has been associ-

ated with the New York School and with Raymond Queneau's Oulipo Group. It was Oulipo who suggested the formal patterns, sestinas and other fugue-like variations, on which he has built his poetic structures, structures that are, as John Ashbery observes, 'both bizarre and deeply moving'.

The best place to start is probably 'Comatas', the extraordinary mixture of concrete poetry, prose poetry and formal elegy that he produced 'immediately after the painful ending of my first marriage ... it was the almost *Lycidas*-like appropriation of pastoral elements from Theocritus and Virgil down to Mallarmé's *L'Après-midi d'un faune* that got me through the process of dealing, however indirectly, with what I could barely face as experience'. The result is the nearest thing I know in contemporary poetry to the *Song of Solomon*:

> Sever me from my appetent mind,
> From the drum's glory, from the Dutch agio
> Of dividends, bananas, and Christ's
> Prayer, not from seduction not
> From the limn of her limbs
>                     nor the way of her waist
> From the air of her hair  and the ease of her
>                                         ears
> From the bow of her elbow  and the shoal of
>                                   her shoulders ...

'Trial Impressions' takes a song from John Dowland's Second Book of Ayres – 'Deare, if you change, Ile never chuse againe' – through thirty variations, recreating not just its argument but its cadence in radically different styles. By Variation XIX the elements of Dowland's conceit – 'Fire heate shall lose and frosts of flames be borne,/ Ayre made to shine as blacke as hell shall prove' – have begun to recur with sinister emphasis – 'an old "flame" now can turn me blue with cold:/Why was the black night burning in your room that winter afternoon?' – and it becomes clear that this game, if it is one, is being played as a way of holding on to sanity: 'Only my image might for a while hover/ On the fringe of that gravity before being sucked after me'.

Mathews is a postmodernist who likes to play on period instruments. But he is postmodern for all that, and with a serious purpose. He is taking the cosmos of classical poetry, with its images of order and continuity, and remaking it in our broken image. At the end of 'Out of Bounds' he repeats the proud boast of Shakespeare's Eighteenth Sonnet: 'So long as men can breathe, or eyes can see,/ So long lives this, and this gives life to thee' only to reverse it and make it into an expression of humility: 'And in that shining you will justify this our last collusion, and/ from it I shall pluck my only survival'.

Look in the 'definitive' anthologies and you will not find **John Mole**. He is one of our unsung masters, capable of writing poems that seem generated naturally out of their own imagery, that accomplish themselves seamlessly and, as it were, selflessly, not an ostentatious word, an unfelt rhythm, an unnecessary effect. *Depending on the Light*, his eighth collection, contains at least a dozen poems of that quality.

Many of them reflect on the experience of ageing oneself and watching the older generation in their decline, negotiated sometimes with dignity, sometimes without:

What he most cares for now
Are oranges (beside his bed
The jordan, sweetly sour,
Afloat with curlicues of peel
Like Chinese lanterns
Drifting there beneath
Stained fingers and the smack
Of restless lips)

It is something of a shock, after the sober truth of these poems, to come upon the remnants of an earlier style, an unquestioning lyricism into which Mole occasionally slips, particularly when lulled by rhyme and metre. The title of 'The Floral Costumier' is enough to warn of what's to come, 'little silken/ arum lilies' that 'drift towards you/ blowing kisses'. The poet's retreat he describes in 'An Island Hut', a 'jaunty, scalloped thinking-cap/ Of corrugated iron' seems altogether too jaunty. But there are also love poems that can stand beside the poems of ageing, poems that have recovered from 'love's amazement', or are slowly recovering it, winning it back, as in 'Revenant', word by word.

Mathews and Mole are two very different poets who have one thing in common: their poetry is self-sufficient and proceeds from the conviction that poetry is a way of thinking in itself. A point worth making at a time when so many people write as if poetry was just a form of stripped-down prose. **Paul Mills**' third collection, *Half Mooon Bay*, takes on some large and crucial themes – the geology of deep time and the discoveries of astrophysics – but rarely takes them beyond the level of the school textbook or the CND pamphlet:

A flick forward or back
runs the tape towards Ice Age or Heat Age.

Between them
this nest of fledgling human,
the world-eater, a few granite boulders.
Stone, wind, ice survive and the tape

plays through them a long time for the life
                    sign.
It seems never, then there's a blip and it's
                    gone.
Stop, reverse, find it again and it's now –
Turf, skylarks. The sea.
Atlantic jet trails. The sun.
A wind of neutrons. The indestructible
                technologies.
A globe of flowers.

Whereas take almost any stanza from **Chris Wallace-Crabbe**'s fourth collection, *Rungs of Time* – 'Galah-coloured dawn/ slouches toward the dry millennium/ thinking there might be/ some long-lost Confucian proverb/explaining that history/ is a three-legged dog' – and you are in a world where the facts are not just presented but imaginatively inhabited.

Many of Paul Mills' poems are based on flights or overland journeys across the Sierra Nevada and the Pacific Coast of America and seem to have come straight from the notebook. He has not allowed time for the transforming play of the imagination. When he does, so much else comes into play with it: the language and the rhythms begin to drive. A long poem like 'Galactic Landscapes' takes the question that Chris Wallace-Crabbe poses in one of his glancing epistemological enquiries – 'Are the rims/ of consciousness/anything like/ the edges of things?' – and does far more with it:

Follow the edge. It is a hill in process,
finned with bushes, it is ice on Titan, the brows
of an ape, feathery storms in blue over Barra ...

It is stones in ocean-time, granite in unvisited
                time,
the ghost of the shaper we think we see but it is
moors and frayed cloud, hammers of wind-
                contusion.
It is an eye with filament-rods aimed at a point
of edge, receptive, shaped ...

Mostly, though, Wallace-Crabbe's less is more, simply because he has learned to wait for the imagination to make its knight's moves. 'What is poetry', he asks, 'but the whole drunken catalogue dancing', and you sense that he does not mind where a poem starts as long as it carries him sideways. He has a scholar's delight in language – 'chine' for the ridge of a mountain, 'stravaging' for his habit of looking about him as he strolls down the street – and an Audenesque gift for tackling serious themes lightly in musical forms.

'Garth McLeod Brooding', a memorable rendition of the middle-aged blues, has some locutions that seem characteristically Australian – 'And the Tassie account has gone right down the gurgler,/ no cause for mirth' – while others would be recognizable anywhere in the global village: 'The fax and the xerox are humming a duet/ in their paperhearted dreaming,/ I feel as old as a beanbag or a Beatle'.

He creates a texture of surprise, setting the colloquial against the highflown, the domestic detail against the scholarly reference. It's a knowing style that tries to cover all its bets: but he's at his best when he risks simplicity, writing in a chastened free verse, as in 'Trace Elements', which touches on the deaths of his father and his son:

> It is at random seasons when the mind
> is full at ease that my father, roundshouldered,
> shuffles along to wait for lights to change
> or my tall son shambles down the footpath
> in a woollen cap, relentlessly unfashionable
> and quiet as a cloud.
>                What do they want?
> Can they be translated?

John Mole takes a short 'Item' from the newspaper and by the lightest of touches, an intermittent rhyme echoing 'lullay, lullay', makes it as haunting as a folksong. **Graham Mort** takes the tale of two young lovers and, across a sequence of seven poems, turns it into an unexceptional short story. In so doing he allows himself the sort of cliché – 'His words circled like moths/ Drawn to her mute, corrosive flame' – that he would probably have avoided if he actually had been working in prose.

Mort has written well in the past but there's something heavy-handed about *Snow from the North*, a sense of misapplied energy. It's as if he has concentrated on the language, creating mimetic effects of a rather predictable kind, rather than on the whole mental act of the poem. As a result, the poem's imagistic life tends to flare up suddenly in unearned effects. 'On Caton Road' is about one motorcyclist coming upon another killed in an accident. The casualty, whom 'cold air' had 'blasted ... seconds ahead' is glimpsed 'lying alone –/ As if you'd sinned', while his helpless attendant, who had been 'kneeling amongst crazed lights', rises and turns 'Towards the locked house of tomorrow/ For which there is no key'. A poem by Ted Hughes suddenly turns into one by Lorca.

For most of the book it is Ted Hughes who wins. Mort has a weakness for the Gothic, which means he is liable to hear 'lost souls clamour in the wiper blades' of the title poem, or to imagine 'Climbing With a Dead Man', an idea that might have worked if he had executed it with any subtlety. Surely in a poem about climbing the last thing you do is come up with lines like 'Questions piton deep into my stone-numb,/ Fissured mind'.

But then Mort is not one to spare us the obvious. Most of his Gulf War and Kurdish refugee poems, of which the blurb makes a great deal, are no more than thumping transcripts of television newsreels. He rarely allows himself a moment of inwardness, such as the one that finally redeems 'Mending his Motorcycle in Wartime':

> At last, unsuspected,
> He found the broken wires,
> Cleaned them, touched them together
> In a scatter of blue sparks:
> The engine fired, joyfully turned
> Then stalled, lying still as his hands
> Moved apart to let silence fall.

Fortunately he does have his Lorca side and this comes uppermost in the final sequence, 'The Red Field', which is spoken in the voices of a pair of twins scarred by sexual abuse, the brother in a mental home and the sister helplessly bonded to him:

> I want to shout out, over and over:
> 'I'm in the red field!
> The red field!'
>
> But her face turns slowly away
> Leaving the moon there,
> Cold on the furrows –
> The million mouths of God.
>
> In the morning,
> In the cold grey morning,
> Birds will break through these windows
>
> And peck me up like corn.

Clarity of image has replaced the muscular language that turns so much of this book, in Dylan Thomas's phrase, into prose with blood-pressure. Perhaps it is simply that Mort has been released by the shorter line and the songlike form. He no longer has to prove that he is writing poetry and, consequently, he is able to write it.

# ➤ *News/Comment*

## New Generation Update

Officially, the New Generation promotion ran from May 3-31st but of course the book-selling process, the schedules of newspapers and journals, the gestation of ideas inspired by such a promotion obey no such cut-off dates. Nevertheless, there are already some facts and figures available that indicate real success. The five Faber authors between them sold 5000 more copies than their average monthly sales before May. In Don Paterson's case, he sold an astonishing 15 times as many copies as usual, Michael Hofmann managed a 9-fold increase, while the already high profile Simon Armitage achieved a four-fold increase, as did Lavinia Greenlaw. Bloodaxe put 8500 of their New Generation books into the shops, and Cape have sold out their 2500-copy editions of David Dabydeen and John Burnside. Another encouraging sign is the response to the Arts Council's Readership Survey. Twenty two thousand forms were printed and inserted into New Generation titles. At the time of writing over 450 have been returned. From the standard return rate expected from insertions this would indicate actual sales out of the bookshops of 10,000-plus by the end of May. For logistical reasons not every title contained a form, so the total sale will be higher.

*Poetry Review* printed 7500 copies, against a standard print run for the last few issues of 4000. Over 3000 were subscribed by bookshops against standing orders of 300. The British Council bought 500 and offered them to their overseas outlets as a shop window of contemporary British poetry. The British Council have ordered a further 200 and report great enthusiasm abroad. The *Review*'s sales have been assisted by many reviews and mentions, especially in the *Observer, Sunday Times, Daily Telegraph, Sunday Telegraph, Spectator, Independent*, and the *Big Issue*.

Despite the fears of some poets, New Generation was never meant simply to promote 20 poets to the exclusion of everyone else. It was intended to give a further twist of the ratchet to the gathering support for poetry, and in this it has been highly successful. Several new projects have either resulted from the network that delivered the New Generation or have been emboldened by its success to be more ambitious. The Forward Prize (publicity by the New Generation's Colman Getty) will be televised by BBC2 on National Poetry Day (October 6th), with the anthology to be published by Faber. National Poetry Day is another William Sieghart initiative, with support from the Poetry Society – for details see the back cover. The *New Statesman & Society* now has a lively and attractive poetry page edited by Adrian Mitchell. On October 2 the South Bank Show will devote an entire programme to the New Generation Poets. And around National Poetry Day the ICA begin a series of four events on poetry's new profile, *Hype, Hype, Hooray*, with *Poetry & Science, Microsoft Words (poetry in the 3-minute culture)*, and *Feuds, Factions, and Fracas* to follow. Then there's Poetry International at the South Bank in November. The autumn promises to be even more exciting than the month of May.

## The Oxford Poetry Chair non-Affair

### *Adam Schwartzman on backing Les Murray as Professor of Poetry and losing*

A few months ago I had an idea of putting together a slate to nominate Les Murray for the Oxford Professorship of Poetry. I thought at the time that no donnish plot could succeed in getting in an Oxford man instead of the outsider; surely 'The Boys' would not risk the embarrassment of turning down so eminent and acclaimed a poet as Murray.

Oh well. It seems as if the Oxford mafia have no shame: James Fenton is the new Professor of Poetry, having won more votes than all the other candidates put together.

But clichés aside, the interesting thing about this election is that donnish plots had nothing to do with the result. Not all of the high-profile academics were Fenton men and women: John Carey's support for Les Murray probably accounts for most of the 90-odd votes that he did get, and Anne Pasternak Slater was prominent in supporting U.A. Fanthorpe as the contest's first female candidate. Except for Alan Brownjohn's manifesto, his press release, and a few innocuous parties, the whole campaign has been a distinctly low key affair.

This is possibly because Oxford MAs don't have to be rounded up into posses by eager campaigners to vote for the 'official' nominee (backed this time by a slate including the heads of four colleges, John Bayley, Iris Murdoch John Fuller, Peter Levi, Anthony Thwaite, Craig Raine, Sir Isaiah Berlin even ...). They just do it naturally. After all, Fenton does live near Oxford and is very well known in University circles. For many MAs, voting for the Oxford man is as obvious as Ted Hughes writing another poem about bones.

This kind of conservatism has made for outrageous selections in the past – the venerable authorities are infamous for once managing to turn down Lowell for Blunden. But if this year's result is a travesty, it is not quite as extreme, and there is no reason for critics to sharpen their claws. What has happened is not surprising; but nor is it especially sinister: the alumni have elected to a university chair a candidate backed by most of the dons and professors; and this candidate – although not as obviously most qualified for the post as the result would suggest – is not lacking in the qualities that a good Professor should have.

On being elected to the post Fenton was pleased at being given the opportunity of putting his ideas down on paper; well, he's left it rather late, but he may be vindicated for taking so long about it if his extensive experience as an arts critic, political correspondent and columnist is put to good use. To those not directly involved with the university the fifteen lectures that Fenton will have to give will be the most important of his duties.

In the end though, you can't help being supported by the senior members of the Oxford establishment even if you could be blamed for writing in the kind of way that pleases them! So, with a tearful glance towards God's representative near Perth, I should say that James Fenton is probably going to do a superb job as far as being involved in university life is concerned. He lives nearby so can, if he wants to, become a kind of poet in residence. Contact with us, the undergraduates, has been an important issue in the campaign, and on more than one occasion Fenton has expressed his willingness to get involved.

I suppose that Fenton as Professor in 1994 might be a little like having Auden in 1936 rather than 1956. But then again, Auden being Auden in the thirties may very well have been more exciting than Auden being Auden in the fifties.

**Adam Schwartzman appears in Carcanet's New Poetries.**

## Prizes on Tap

The poetry prize season now seems to go on forever. Summer is the time of the Society of Authors Awards, which this year disbursed £90,000. Helen Dunmore adds to her increasingly impressive list of achievements with the £5000 McKitterick prize for a first novel by a writer over 40, for her first novel *Zennor in Darkness* (Penguin). Jackie Kay won a Somerset Maugham Award and the Gregory Awards went to Julia Copus (see p.73) and Alice Oswald (£6000 each) and £5000 each to Steven Blyth, Kate Clanchy, and Giles Goodland. The Geoffrey Faber Memorial Prize (£1000) alternates between poetry and fiction.

New Generation poet John Burnside is this year's winner for *Feast Days* (Secker & Warburg).

This year's Forward Prize shows further development. The prizes remain the same (£10,000 for the best collection; £5000 for best first collection; £1000 for best poem in a magazine), but, as already mentioned, the ceremony will be televised on BBC2 on National Poetry Day. This year's judges are Cressida Connolly (chair), Jean 'Binta' Breeze, Carol Ann Duffy, John Gross, and Alexandra Shulman.

Poets who have won Arts Council Writers' Awards worth £7000 each are: Jacqueline Brown, Stephen Duncan, U. A. Fanthorpe, Mimi Khalvati, Stephen Knight, David Morley, and Gerard Woodward.

## Report on No. 28: Movie Verse

**We asked for speech bubbles and/or captions for the classic Bogart/Bergman still from Casablanca.**

Several of you were moved to write poems rather than captions, and these were in fact the best entries.

### Keats on Casablanca
The poetry of love is never dead:
Here's Bogey with his wry, laconic smile,
And Bergman lifting her well-tailored head
To meet his eyes – love 1940s style.

'As time goes by', these lovers laid in earth
Still live in sound and motion on the screen,
And Casablanca is their love's rebirth,
Annihilating all the years between.

If Shakespeare had the cinematic art
At his command, he'd have immortalised
That lovely youth, the darling of his heart
In celluloid – and we'd have paid the price.

Would he still need those sonnets to express
The transience of love and loveliness?
**Joan Smith**

## No. 30: Hit Singles

'Funeral Blues', rediscovered 60 years after its writing, has transformed Auden into a truly popular poet. Nominations wanted for poems lurking in other *oeuvres* that might work the same trick. Up to four 1995 *Writers' & Artists' Yearbooks* to be won; deadline: Oct 1.

# *Letters*

## Talking About the New Generation

Dear Peter,

I appreciate your special issue, New Generation Poets very much (Vol 84 No 1). Except for one thing: how can Michael Hofmann, in his review of Zbigniew Herbert's *Mr Cogito* intimate that this excellent poet would have been closer to the Nobel Prize if he was more translated into English and more often published in America? This is nonsense.

The Nobel Prize is awarded by the Swedish Academi in Stockholm, and members of this venerable institution know the works of Zbigniew Herbert very well, as his poetry has been translated into Swedish several times throughput the years.

Michael Hofmann seems to overestimate the importance of the English language in the question of getting the Nobel Prize. Throughout the years this most important literary prize has been awarded to writers not much known in the USA, such as Jaroslav Seifert (1984), Vincente Aleixandre (1977) or Eyvind Johnson (1974). The Swedish Academi makes its own choice.

Of course the English language is important for a writer. But if he wants to get the Nobel Prize it should not be of any significance to write in – or be translated into – English. In fact the Swedish language is more important in this case. And it has to be outstanding poetry as well.

Yours sincerely,

**Neil Hav**
Copenhagen
Denmark


Dear Peter Forbes

I much enjoyed the *Poetry Review* Special Issue – New Generation Poets, which encouraged me to go out and buy some more books. Pauline Stainer, Susan Wicks, Sarah Maguire, and Elizabeth Garrett were the poets who especially appealed to me. Moniza Alvi, too, but, alas, Swindon did not have *The Country at my Shoulder* in stock when I was looking. Sheer chance, I think, that the ones I liked best were women...

Yours sincerely,

**Diana Stow,**
Faringdon

Dear Peter,

Amid the welter of hype in your New Generation Poets issue, two quotations worth remembering: 'The poet must always keep away from crowds and their interests' (J. B. Yeats, in a letter to his son, W. B.). 'They don't like poetry; they like something else, but they like to think they like poetry' (W. B. Yeats).

**William Cookson**
Editor, *Agenda*

## Harpur Defended

Dear Sir,

I must challenge Sean O'Brien's review of James Harpur's *A Vision of Comets* in the *Poetry Review* Special Issue, Spring 1994. It is unfair of O'Brien to single out for comment the failings in one poem, 'Tallis: Spem in Alium', without drawing attention to better and more coherent poems in the fifty-odd poem collection such as 'Cretan Easter' or 'Eos', with its wonderful affirmation in the final line. The title poem 'A Vision of Comets' is one of the most arresting poems I remember reading.

As for his musings on the possible existence of a modern day 'community of religious poets', has Sean so lost his common touch as to suppose that such a community ever did *not* exist? This makes his cheap jibe about James Harpur's Gregory Award even less worthy. One could point out that the winner of the 3rd prize in the 1993 National Poetry Competition is also a one-time Gregory Award recipient. Perhaps she used unleaded petrol.

Yours sincerely,

**Robert Butt**
Chislehurst

## Radio Three Lives

Dear Sir,

In the belief that poets are energetic quarriers, I would like to correct John Whitworth's article on poetry and broadcasting (Vol 83 No 4), which dismissed Radio 3's lack of poetic substance. Flip through *Radio Times* and you will see Thom Gunn, Maura Dooley, Les Murray reading poems throughout a week, anthologies of poets to coincide with the 30s season, gems dug up by Peter Porter from the archives.

And, on their way, programmes of poets on earlier poets; a new series of poetry in action – where poetry plugs into the world; a 45-minute commissioned poem from Simon Armitage, all produced by Fiona McLean, whose Poet of the Month on Radio 3 is to be published as an anthology by Carcanet. Different and complementary to the excellent work done by Susan Roberts on Radio 4.

So the spirit of the Third Programme lives, and is adapted to the schedules of a music-based Radio 3. Should there be more? Of course, let's work towards it. John Whitworth's article will help.

Yours sincerely,

**Richard Bannerman**

Editor, Documentary Features,
Arts, Science & Features Radio

## Vuk from the Woods

Dear Peter,

I should like to respond to the short review of *Red knight: Serbian Women's Songs* (Menard King's) (Vol 83 No 3), even if the brevity of this notice scarcely seems to warrant a response. First, as a matter of accuracy, it was not myself, but my collaborator Tomislav Longinovic who talked of these poems as 'an antidote to the poison of national rhetoric presented by (male) politicians in Yugoslavia'. Not that I would dissociate myself from that point of view. What is clear is that your reviewer was more interested in making a point, than in attentively reading the texts or the introductions to the texts. Thus the reviewer picks one, somewhat untypical poem whose resonances disturb him and ignores the rest. Of course, in the current mode, no attempt is made to take into account the historical circumstances. For instance, while drawing attention to the atrocities committed against Muslims by Serbs, your reviewer evidently ignores the fact that the Turks governed the South Slav lands for centuries. As ought to be obvious, the folk poet in question was referring directly to Turks, not to Islamized Serbs. Furthermore, since the context of the poem itself is not supplied it is misrepresented. After all, the Turkish women in the poem who are screwed by 'Vuk from the Woods' are scarcely portrayed as victims, and the poem concludes with the Bey's young wife's sexuality triumphant!

I find it disturbing that increasingly reviewers seem unable to consider works in their historical context. The tendency is to relate them immediately to the present circumstances and use them rhetorically to make some point or other. Not to do this, it appears, is to run the risk of being considered naive or, worse still, an apologist for some heresy or other. In compiling *Red Night* Prof. Longinovic and I had hoped to shed another (almost proto-Reichan!) light on the nationalist or tribal aspirations of the contending forces in former Yugoslavia – and not only there. I suppose we were hoping for too much and therein lies our naivety.

Yours sincerely,

**Daniel Weissbort**

Iowa City
USA


# Writers' & Artists' Yearbook 1994

**87th Edition**

*The indispensable reference book for poets, writers and anyone involved in creative work.*

**660 pages paperback**
**£9.99**

**A & C BLACK**